FLOWERS

of the

WORLD

Maurice Lecoufle's orchids are world famous. In his greenhouses just outside Paris, he acclimatized
and propagated some extremely rare species which have been exported all over the world.
Apart from his great skill as a botanist, he had an exceedingly generous nature and was always ready to help.
Many of the wonderful orchid photographs in this book were produced by him.

Maurice Lecoufle died in October 1994. We would like to dedicate this book to him.

Copyright © 1996 by Copyright, Paris

Published by Longmeadow Press, 311 Maynard, Ann Arbor, MI 48104.

Cover and interior design by Anne Fleming
Editor: Frédérique Crestin-Billet
English language edition: Cathy Muscat, International Editions

Colour reproduction : SCAN 4, Spain

ISBN : 0-681-10488-0

Printed in Spain

First Longmeadow Press Edition

0 9 8 7 6 5 4 3 2 1

FLOWERS

of the

WORLD

— ❈ —

Michel Viard

LP LONGMEADOW PRESS

CONTENTS

Flowers of
the tropical forest

✳

The regions between the Tropic of Cancer and the Tropic of Capricorn are both the hottest and the most humid in the world. Here, the diurnal and nocturnal temperatures are nearly identical, seasons do not exist, and plants thrive and flower all year long. From the tops of tall trees drenched in sunlight, down to the forest floor hidden under dark undergrowth, plantlife flourishes everywhere – over 1500 different species of flowers and 750 types of trees have been counted in an area measuring just twelve acres in the Monteverde forest in Costa Rica. Despite this exuberance of growth, the tropical forest is a fragile place. Every species is linked to another. Cutting one tree means death to hundreds of ferns, moss, orchids, and creepers that live on the trunk and branches. The newly-exposed light pours down on species accustomed to darkness. Fragile soil loses protection and is carried away unrelentingly by rainwater. Homes are destroyed belonging to dozens of birds and hundreds of insects which carry pollen from flower to flower, maintaining the continuity of plantlife. Twenty years ago, specialists estimated that tropical forests house half of all animal and vegetable species in the world. They calculated that three million species were still undiscovered. Today, scientists agree that figure is more likely ten million, of which 90% are hidden in hot and humid jungles.

Those numbers are high. And it raises a troubling question: Will man have the time to identify and study all the species when tropical forests are being destroyed at the rate of 74 acres a minute?

Opposite : *Dendrobium cruentum.*
Family : Orchidaceae (Burma–Malasia).

Left: *Ipomoea tricolor.* Family : Convolvulaceae (Mexico).

1 *Masdevallia picturata*. Family : Orchidaceae (Ecuador). 2 *Masdevallia robledorum*. Family : Orchidaceae (Colombia).
3 *Dracula vampira*. Family : Orchidaceae (Ecuador). 4 *Dracula chimaera*. Family : Orchidaceae (Colombia). 5 *Masdevallia coccinea*.
Family : Orchidaceae (Colombia–Peru). 6 *Masdevallia caudata*. Family : Orchidaceae (Colombia–Venezuela).

Opposite: *Masdevallia veitchiana*. Family : Orchidaceae (Peru).

Just south of the equator is a vast, mountainous area covered in thick and impenetrable forest. Here lies the land that time forgot.
This mountain range known as El Condor which forms the frontier between Peru and Ecuador, is inaccessible and politically ill-defined.
Only a few missionaries, the Jivaros in particular, who had come to convert the Indians to Christianity, showed an interest in this region.
Father Andreetta had gone to the rescue of the last tribes of the cordillera and discovered that the forests contained millions of species of
orchids, especially Masdevillias and Draculas, most of which were unknown. With the help of some American botanists, he endeavoured to
persuade the two bordering countries to set up the first world sanctuary for orchids in El Condor.

1 *Passiflora coriacea*. Family : Passifloraceae (Mexico–Peru). **2** Blue Passion Flower *Passiflora caerulea*. Family : Passifloraceae (Brazil). **3** Violet Passion Flower *Passiflora violacea*. Family : Passifloraceae (Rio de Janeiro, Brazil). **4** *Passiflora cymbarina*. Family : Passifloraceae (Ecuador).

Opposite : Purple Passion Flower *Passiflora edulis*. Family : Passifloraceae (Brazil).

Following pages : Queen of the night *Selenicereus grandiflorus*. Family : Cactaceae (Jamaica).

During the hot summer nights the smell of vanilla fills the air of the Jamaican tropical forests. The "Queen of the night" unfurls her huge white flowers which span more than 35 centimetres. The perfume that these flowers produce is one of the most powerful in the plant kingdom. It penetrates the forest for miles around and attracts the bats whose task it is to pollinate them. This plant is a cactus. The fine square stems, dotted with thorns, wrap around the trees of the forest thanks to the aerial roots. Just one plant can produce stems over 100 metres long. Sadly, the "Queen of the night" has a short reign and wilts after just a few hours.

1 *Dendrobium brymerianum*. Family : Orchidaceae (Burma–Laos–Thailand). **2** *Paphiopedilum rothschildianum*. Family : Orchidaceae (Borneo, but only on Mount Kinabalu). **3** *Odontoglossum bictoniense*. Family : Orchidaceae (Mexico–Guatemala). **4** *Oncidium papilio*. Family : Orchidaceae (Ecuador–Peru). **5** *Brassia longissima*. Family : Orchidaceae (Costa Rica–Panama). **6** *Paphiopedilum sukhakulii*. Family : Orchidaceae (Thailand).

Opposite : *Epidendrum ilense*. Family : Orchidaceae (Ecuador).

In 1976 a group of botanists in Ecuador spotted three plants of an unknown orchid growing on a fallen tree. It was named *Epidendrum ilense*, but before even being classified as a near extinct species it disappeared from its environment which was devastated by bulldozers and chainsaws. Of the three salvaged plants, one went to America, one to England and the third to France, where a programme of micropropagation was applied enabling the plant to multiply and flower.

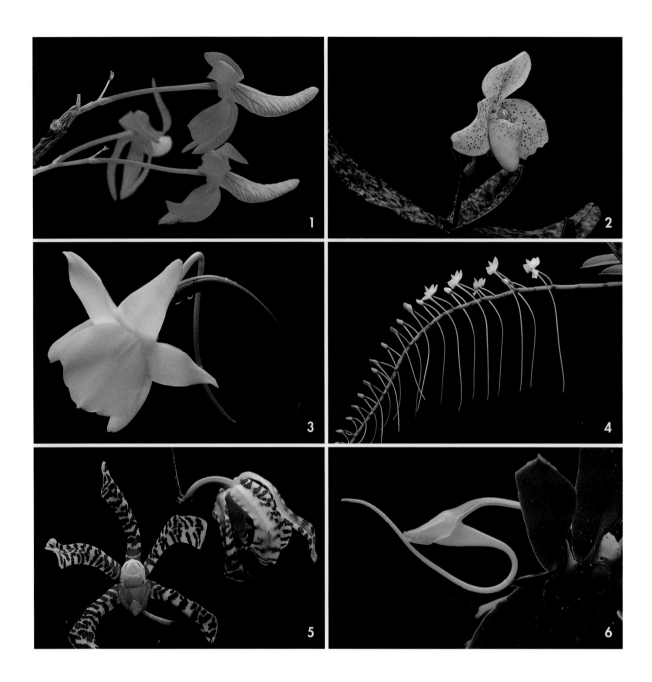

1 *Dendrobium unicum*. Family : Orchidaceae (New Guinea). **2** *Paphiopedilum concolor*. Family : Orchidaceae (Burma).
3 *Angraecum magdalenae*. Family : Orchidaceae (Madagascar). **4** *Aerangis cryptodon*. Family : Orchidaceae (Uganda–Kenya).
5 *Arachnis flos-aeris*. Family : Orchidaceae (Sumatra–Java). **6** *Angraecum compactum*. Family : Orchidaceae (Madagascar).

Opposite : *Angraecum sesquipedale*. Family : Orchidaceae (Madagascar).

In 1850, in Madagascar, Darwin discovered an orchid with white and waxy petals, *Angraecum sesquipedale*, with a 40-centimetre spur.
At the base of this tube is a sweet liquid. Darwin surmised that this nectar was clearly destined for the orchid's pollinator and maintained
that there must be an insect in the Madagascan forest with a 40-centimetre proboscis, in addition to which it must be nocturnal because
the *Angaraecum* is fragrant only by night. Darwin was ridiculed by entomologists as no one believed it possible that such an insect could
exist. Fifty years later the *Xanthopan morgani predicta*, was discovered. This nocturnal hawk-moth has a strange coil on the front of its
head. Attracted by the smell, the hawk-moth is drawn to the orchid and the coil on its head unfurls to a length of 40 centimetres. We
know today that each of the the 200 species of *Angraecum* has its own hawk-moth. The length of the proboscis always corresponds
exactly to the length of the orchid's spur – a perfect example of the inseparable couple.

1 *Jacobinia chrysostephana*. Family : Acanthaceae (Brazil). This plant originates from Jacobinia, a Brazilian town in the state of Bahia.
2 *Aeschynanthus speciosus.* Family : Gesneriaceae (Java). **3** *Pachystachys lutea.* Family : Acanthaceae (Peru). **4** *Crossandra nilotica.*
Family : Acanthaceae (India–Sri Lanka). **5** Zebra Plant *Aphelandra squarrosa*. Family : Acanthaceae (Brazil). **6** *Calathea crocata.*
Family : Marantaceae (Brazil). Indians use *Calathea* leaves for weaving baskets. *Kalathos* is Greek for "basket".

Opposite : *Gloriosa rothschildiana*. Family : Liliaceae (Kenya–Uganda).

The *Gloriosa* starts off by growing straight. Once it has sprouted four or five leaves, its stem begins to bend and curl in search of support.
Tiny tendrils appear on the tips of the new leaves which, with the slightest contact, attach themselves to the branches of neighbouring
plants. At this stage in its growth, the stem of the *Gloriosa* will cease to curl, the tendrils having taken over the job of finding new props to
wrap around and use for support. When it reaches maturity, the adult leaves are thick and no longer have hooks. The plant then flowers.
The *Gloriosa* was highly sought after by the indigenous hunters of the tropical African forest, not for its beautiful flowers, but for the
highly toxic bulbous root, rich in alkaloids, which they used in the preparation of poison for the tips of their arrows.

1 *Tibouchina semidecandra.* Family : Melastomaceae (Brazil). **2** *Hoya multiflora.* Family : Asclepiadaceae (Malacca–Malaysia–Borneo).
3 *Begonia metallica.* Family : Begoniaceae (Bahia, Brazil). **4** *Solanum pyracanthum.* Family : Solanaceae (Madagascar).
5 *Ixora macrothyrsa.* Family : Rubiaceae (Sumatra). **6** *Hoya bella.* Family : Asclepiadaceae (India).

Opposite : *Hoya carnosa.* Family : Asclepiadaceae (China).

At the hottest time of day, the white and waxy flowers of the *Hoya* plant release translucent drops of nectar into the air which are instantly gathered up by bees or ants. There are more than fifty species of the *Hoya* growing in the forests of Malaysia, India and Australia. The majority of them are lianas. When they are still young, *Hoya* plants, with their thick and fleshy stems and leaves, have the characteristics of succulents. As they mature, the stems become more woody and the leaves grow thinner. All these species display the effects of variegation; they are scattered with white spots and their leaves are often twisted.

Following pages : *Setcreasea purpurea.* Family : Commelinaceae (Mexico).

20

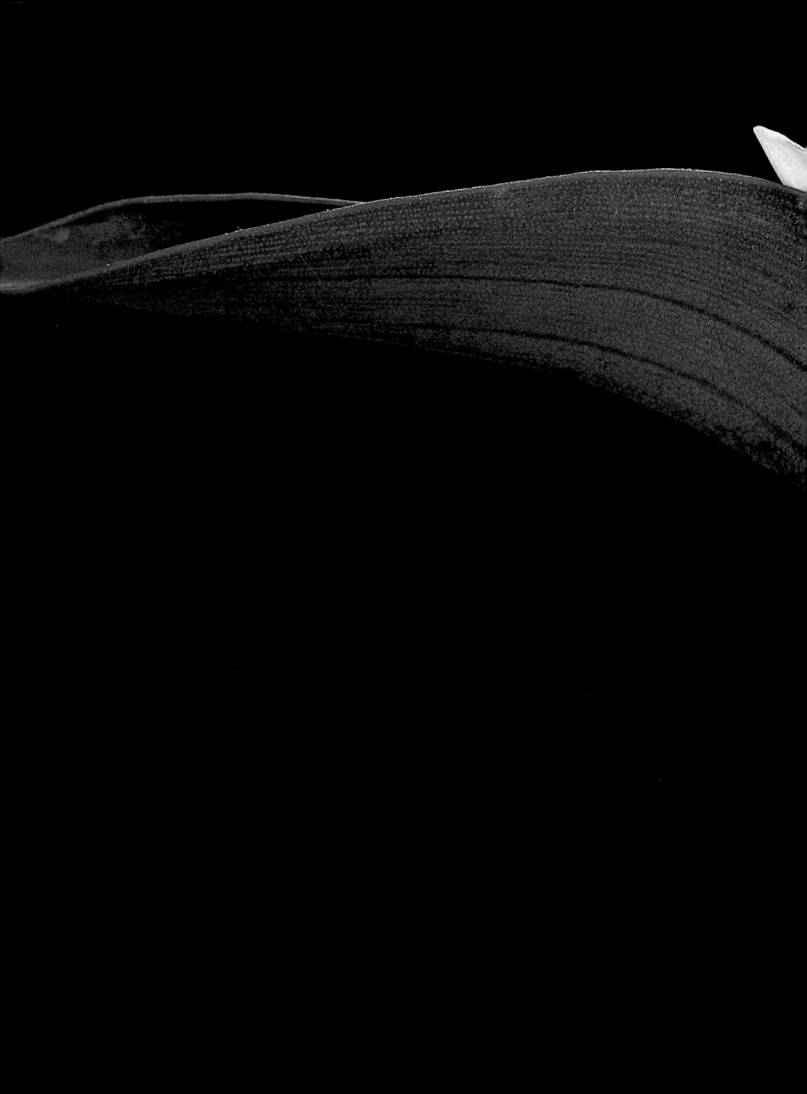

1 *Bulbophyllum lobii*. Family : Orchidaceae (Bali). **2** *Cymbidiella rhodochila*. Family : Orchidaceae (Madagascar). **3** *Brassavola nodosa*. Family : Orchidaceae (Panama). **4** *Phragmipedium besseae*. Family : Orchidaceae (Ecuador). **5** *Cymbidium finlaysonianum*. Family : Orchidaceae (Philippines–Malaysia–Sumatra). **6** *Dendrobium crystallinum*. Family : Orchidaceae (Burma).

Opposite : *Catasetum pileatum*. Family : Orchidaceae (Venezuela).

The pollen produced by the *Catasetum* plant is all concentrated on a single stamen where it is divided into two clumps or polliniums. The insects that visit these plants are treated rather violently by their hosts. The male flower has a mechanism that is triggered at the slightest touch and catapults the two polliniums onto the insect's head, stunning and often killing it. But despite such brutal treatment, the *Catasteum* are never short of visiting insects, especially males, who brave these dangers for a few drops of the precious substance which gives off a strong smell of mint. If they escape unscathed, they disperse the perfume into the air with their wings to mark out their territory and attract their mates.

1 *Solandra nitida*. Family : Solanaceae (Jamaica–Mexico). As these magnificent, coconut-scented flowers mature, their colour changes from pale to golden yellow, hence the name "Golden chalice" **2** Frangipani *Plumeria acutifolia*. Family : Apocynaceae (Mexico). The smell of these flowers is reminiscent of frangipane, a blend of civet and amber **3** Gardenia *Gardenia jasminoides*. Family : Rubiaceae (China). Cultivated for the heady perfume contained within its flowers, the gardenia is also used in China for medicinal purposes. Known locally as "zhi zi", it is used in poultices applied to sprains and dislocations. **4** *Spathiphyllum patinii*. Family : Araceae (Colombia). **5** *Petrea kohautiana*. Family : Verbenaceae (Panama). **6** *Clusia rosea*. Family : Guttiferae (Panama–Venezuela).

Opposite : Bougainvillea *Bougainvillea glabra*. Family : Nyctaginaceae (Brazil).

1 *Vriesea psittacina*. Family : Bromeliaceae (Brazil). **2** *Aechmea recurvata*. Family : Bromeliaceae (Uruguay–Brazil).
3 *Billbergia nutans*. Family : Bromeliaceae (Uruguay–Argentina). **4** *Aechmea nudicaulis*. Family : Bromeliaceae (Brazil).
5 *Tillandsia cyanea*. Family : Bromeliaceae (Ecuador). **6** *Aechmea chantinii*. Family : Bromeliaceae (Venezuela–Peru).

Opposite : *Aechmea fasciata*. Family : Bromeliaceae (Brazil).

The majority of species belonging to the Bromeliaceae family thrive without ever coming into contact with the ground. Like orchids, they are epiphytes and have evolved to such an extent that they do not rely on their roots for survival. They store the nutrients needed for growth in their leaves which are covered with minuscule hairs that capture both food and moisture. Many compensate for the lack of ground compost by using their tightly overlapping leaves, which spiral around the stem, in such a way that the centre of the plant becomes a watertight reservoir, where rainwater and the organic particles it carries collect. This natural foodstore contains a whole world of living organisms which reproduce and die: microscopic aquatic plants, insects, everything that attracts frogs and hummingbirds, the ideal pollinators for Bromelias. These "bird-flies" are attracted by the plants' bright colours. The tiny flowers are heavily scented and nestle among bright red, yellow or variegated leaves arranged along scapes or in rosettes.

1 Clove Tree *Eugenia caryophyllus.* Family : Myrtaceae (the Moluccas). The cloves themselves are the flower buds that have been dried.
2 *Pavonia multiflora.* Family : Malvaceae (Brazil). **3** Lobster Claws *Heliconia wagneriana.* Family : Heliconiaceae (Costa Rica).
Large scapes protect the green flowers which lie in shallow ponds where flies thrive and multiply, attracting hummingbirds who
feed off them and pollinate the heliconia. **4** *Monstera deliciosa.* Family : Araceae (Guatemala–Mexico). The inflorescence of this plant
develops into a delicious fruit which tastes like a cross between a strawberry and a banana. **5** Ginger *Zingiber spectabile.*
Family : Zingiberaceae (Malaysia). **6** Red Ginger *Alpinia purpurea.* Family : Zingiberaceae (the Moluccas–New Caledonia).

Opposite : *Nidularium innocentii.* Family : Bromeliaceae (Brazil).

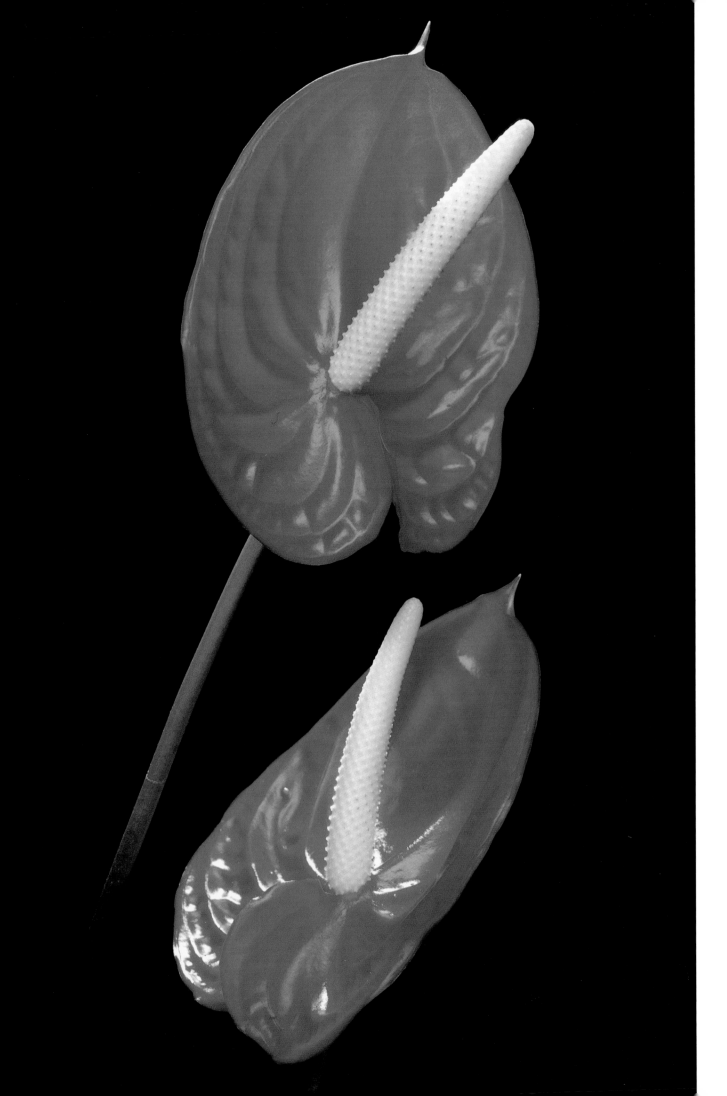

1 *Asclepias currassavica*. Family : Asclepiadaceae (Brazil–Argentina). **2** *Ceropegia distincta*. Family : Asclepiadaceae (Malaysia–India). **3** *Periploca laevigata*. Family : Asclepiadaceae (Africa). **4** *Ceropegia stapeliiformis*. Family : Asclepiadaceae (Malaysia–India). **5** *Ceropegia ampliata*. Family : Asclepiadaceae (Africa). **6** *Alocasia sanderiana*. Family : Araceae (Philippines).

The corollas of the *Ceropegia* are covered at their very tips with tiny hairs that move with the wind. This downy layer attracts aphids which mistake it for a bunch of their fellow creatures. The irresistible perfume lures them into the flower, where they discover there's no nectar inside. But it's too late: the walls of the flowers are covered with more fine hairs, which point downwards, making it impossible for the aphids to fly back out again. In their struggle to escape, they get covered in pollen and are released, if they have not died of exhaustion, only when the flower wilts a few days later. The *Asclepias* is just as sadistic. When wasps come to collect their nectar, they land on the stamens which contract on contact and trap them. Only the strongest manage to tear themselves off and fly away covered with pollen. The majority die on the flower. *Alocasias*, on the other hand, take snails as their victims. They are attracted by the strong odour of decomposition and slither along the pollen-covered spathe. The fine powder is an irritant which drives them away to a second *Alocasia*, the flowers of which eject a corrosive liquid onto them. Writhing in pain, the snail reluctantly deposits the pollen it picked up on its first visit.

Opposite : *Anthurium andreanum*. Family : Araceae (Colombia).

33

Flowers of
the temperate forest

✳

The major temperate forest zones of the world are divided between Europe, central China, Japan and North America. Temperate forests are rare south of the equator and are only found in the southernmost reaches of Africa and South America. Even though the climatic conditions vary considerably from one region to another, the structure of most of these forests is quite similar in the Northern Hemisphere. The same species are often found: oak and beech trees over-hang a stratum of maple and birch trees which shelter a ground soil rich in herbaceous plants. Vegetation lives according to the rhythm of the seasons. As winter approaches, the majority of trees shed their leaves. In the spring, before new leaves begin to sprout, a multitude of flowers pop up through the well-lit soil beneath the branches of the trees. In summer, the undergrowth is shaded by the trees and so the vegetation stays fresh and moist. In autumn, the decomposition of fallen leaves provides a rich fertilizer for the forest floor, helping a new cycle begin.

Deciduous trees are always highly favoured in the natural evolution of the temperate forest. Coniferous trees are the pioneers, but they are quickly replaced first by birch, then oak and finally beech trees, which are the undisputed champions of the forest. The coniferous tree has been chased back towards inhospitable zones, north of the 55th parallel, where the air is intensely cold and violent winds blow (the largest forest in the world, found in Siberia, is made up almost entirely of pine and larch trees).

The forests we are familiar with today have been shaped by man and are far from being natural. The forestry industry prefers replanting with pine and other types of fast-growing coniferous trees. These trees, defeated in the past, now make up the majority of our temperate forests.

Opposite : Primrose Officinal *Primula officinalis.* Family : Primulaceae.

Left : *Trillium sessile.* Family : Trilliaceae (North America).

35

1 Wild Madder *Rubia peregrina*. Family : Rubiaceae. **2** Wayfaring Tree *Viburnum lantana*. Family : Caprifoliceae.
3 *Deutzia gracilis*. Family : Saxifragaceae (Japan). **4** Bladder Nut *Staphylea colchica*. Family : Staphyleaceae (Russia).
5 Hawthorn *Crataegus oxyacanthoides*. Family : Rosaceae. **6** Hemp Agrimony *Eupatorium cannabinum*. Family : Compositae.

Hawthorn is reputed to ward off both lightning and snakes. Some believe that hawthorn is never struck by lightning because it was the bush under which Mary slept on her flight to Egypt. In central France many farmers plant hawthorn branches in manure on May 1, supposedly to keep snakes at bay. In years gone by young men would plant a hawthorn bush in flower by the house of the girl they loved.

Legend has it that injured stags search for hemp agrimony to heal their wounds and another old wives' tale maintains that this plant is the perfect remedy for snake bites. This doesn't seem so far-fetched when you consider that South American Indians use a similar species (*Eupatorium crenatum*) to treat scorpion bites. Plants from the *Eupatorium* genus contain eupatorine, which is a powerful alkaloid.

Opposite : Large Cuckoo-pint *Arum italicum*. Family : Araceae.

1 Giant Bellflower *Campanula latifolia*. Family : Campanulaceae. **2** Large Self-heal *Brunella grandiflora*.
Family : Labiatae. **3** Lungwort *Pulmonaria officinalis*. Family : Boraginaceae. **4** Comfrey *Symphytum officinale*. Family : Boraginaceae.
5 Lousewort *Pedicularis silvatica*. Family : Scrophulariaceae. **6** Sweet Violet *Viola odorata*. Family : Violaceae. Since the 5th century BC,
these flowers have been made into crowns used to combat drunkenness. Saint Hildegarde prescribed the use of its leaves as a cure for
melancolia. The plant is also widely used in the perfume industry, as its root contains a wonderful scent.

Opposite : Purple Toothwort *Lathræa clandestina*. Family : Scrophulariaceae.

Toothwort, which grows in damp and leafy woods, is a unique species of the plant kingdom as it is both a parasite and a carnivore.
The flower is cup-shaped and has a spring at its centre that can jettison mature seeds several feet away. If the seed becomes attached to the
root of a birch or elm, it germinates and pushes out suckers which attach it to the tree from which it feeds. Hidden under the earth,
it spreads all around its host and grows into a dense network of white and scaly roots. These underground stems trap minute creatures that
live in the soil. Strengthened by these nutrients, the toothwort then pushes its way up out of the soil and flowers.

Following pages : Dog Rose *Rosa canina*. Family : Rosaceae.

1 Privet *Ligustrum vulgare*. Family : Oleaceae. **2** Elder *Sambucus ebulus*. Family : Caprifoliceae. One day a rich blind man wanted to buy a piece of land, so he mounted his mule and set off with his manservant. When they reached their destination, he asked his servant to tie the mule to an elder. "But there isn't an elder in sight" replied the servant. "Well that means the land's no good" said the blind man and headed straight home. **3** Holly *Ilex aquifolium*. Family : Aquifoliaceae. **4** Box *Buxus sempervirens*. Family : Buxaceae. **5** Traveller's Joy or Old Man's Beard *Clematis vitalba*. Family : Ranunculaceae. Clematis is the only species of creeper to be found in Europe. It is in fact highly toxic. When the leaves are crushed, the properties released into the air can cause the face to swell for several hours. Beggars used to use it to their advantage: by rubbing the liquid from freshly crushed leaves over their faces they caused facial ulcers that were meant to make passers-by feel so sorry for them that they would hand over money – which is why it is sometimes called the "beggar's plant".
6 Blackthorn, Sloe *Prunus spinosa*. Family : Rosaceae.

Opposite : Butcher's Broom *Ruscus aculeatus*. Family : Liliaceae.

Commonly found in dense undergrowth, butcher's broom is composed of spiky evergreen bushes. What appear to be leaves are really modified branches (cladodes), the true leaves being reduced to minute thin scales at their bases. The small flowers produced from the centre of the cladode are succeeded by bright red berries in winter (used during the Second World War as a coffee substitute).

1 Sessile Oak *Quercus sessiliflora*. Family : Fagaceae. **2** Common Ash *Fraxinus excelsior*. Family : Oleaceae.
3 Common White Birch *Betula alba*. Family : Betulaceae. **4** Common Hornbeam *Carpinus betulus*. Family : Corylaceae.
5 Common Chestnut *Castanea vulgaris*. Family : Fagaceae. **6** Common Lime *Tilia vulgaris*. Family : Tiliaceae.

Opposite : Walnut *Juglans regia*. Family : Juglandaceae (Caucasus–China).

The walnut is one of the most useful trees to man. Its edible nuts are very nutritious and have endless uses in cooking. They are also used to make wine or liqueur and are prized for their sweet flavoursome oil. Walnut wood is considered by cabinet-makers to be one of the best because it finishes well, has a pleasing grain and lasts for years. The walnut husk is also a valuable element in homeopathy as it is a key ingredient in the tincture used to treat lymphatic complaints. Veterinary surgeons daub horses and dogs with its crushed green leaves to keep ticks and fleas at bay. But despite its beneficence, the walnut is not the most sociable of plants. Its roots emit a substance that is toxic to surrounding plantlife. There are many old wives' tales surrounding the walnut. It is said that if you sit under a walnut tree, you'll get pneumonia, and throwing a stone at its trunk is meant to ward off bad luck.

1 Horse-chestnut *Aesculus hippocastanum*. Family : Hippocastanaceae (Albania–Greece). Horse-chestnut blossoms are white and grouped along straight spikes. There is a little yellow spot at the base of each corolla which attracts bees. Once the flower is pollinated, this yellow spot turns red. Because bees cannot distinguish red from black they are drawn only to the unfertilized flowers. **2** Bull Bay *Magnolia grandiflora*. Family : Magnoliaceae (Virginia, United States). **3** False Acacia *Robinia pseudoacacia*. Family : Leguminosae (eastern United States). **4** Bird Cherry *Prunus padus*. Family : Rosaceae. **5** Sugar Maple *Acer saccharum*. Family : Aceraceae (Canada–United States). The maple leaf is the Canadian national symbol. **6** *Paulownia tomentosa*. Family : Scrophulariaceae (China–Japan)

Opposite: Chinese Almond Tree *Prunus triloba*. Family : Rosaceae (China).

Following pages : *Pleione formosana*. Family : Orchidaceae (China–Formosa–Tibet).

46

1 Man Orchid *Aceras anthropophorum*. Family : Orchidaceae. **2** Narrow-leaved Helleborine *Cephalanthera longifolia*. Family : Orchidaceae. **3** Giant Orchid *Barlia robertiana*. Family : Orchidaceae (France–Canary Islands). **4** Lesser Butterfly Orchid *Platanthera bifolia*. Family : Orchidaceae (France–Russia–Switzerland). **5** Violet Limodore *Limodorum abortivum*. Family : Orchidaceae. **6** Bird's-nest Orchid *Neottia nidus-avis*. Family : Orchidaceae (Europe).

The bird's-nest orchid is a saprophytic plant, which means that it feeds from the organic waste of other decomposing vegetation. It attaches itself to the roots of beech trees and grows from a ball of roots that looks like a bird's nest (hence the name). The stem is lined with numerous little brown and yellow flowers which attract tiny insects. When the cold weather sets in, the orchid seems to sense that pollinators will become scarce, and so stops growing stems, and withdraws its inflorescence into the humus where, unseen, its flowers self-pollinate.

Opposite : *Bletilla striata*. Family : Orchidaceae (China–Japan–Tibet).

1 Burdock *Lappa communis*. Family : Compositae. **2** Common Stork's-bill *Erodium cicutarium*. Family : Geraniaceae. **3** Hedge Woundwort *Stachys silvatica*. Family : Labiatae. **4** Bell Heather *Erica cinerea*. Family : Ericaceae. **5** Ground Ivy *Glechoma hederacea*. Family : Labiatae. **6** Common Heather *Calluna vulgaris*. Family : Ericaceae.

Opposite : Foxglove *Digitalis purpurea*. Family : Scrophulariaceae.

The foxglove flowers during the second and last years of its life. Its petals are perfectly adapted to the visiting bumble bees who come to collect its nectar. They are covered in white specks on the inside which guide the bees right down to the sweet liquid and reproductive organs. Once fertilized, the flower produces tiny velvet balls that contain thousands of minuscule seeds which are carried off by the wind. If consumed, however, the flowers and leaves are poisonous. In spite of this fact, foxgloves are one of the plants most abundantly used in modern pharmacy. No synthetic substitute has yet been developed that can substitue the glucosides it produces which are used in the treatment of heart conditions.

1 Dog's-tooth Violet *Erythronium dens-canis*. Family : Liliaceae. **2** Downy Woundwort *Stachys germanica*.
Family : Labiatae. **3** Fetid Horehound *Ballota foetida*. Family : Labiatae. **4** Bastard Balm *Melittis melissophyllum*.
Family : Labiatae. **5** Honeysuckle *Lonicera caprifolium*. Family : Caprifoliceae. **6** *Trillium grandiflorum*.
Family : Trilliaceae (North America, national symbol of Quebec).

In the spring, a dozen different species of *Trillium* pop up in their thousands across the forest floors of North America. Three is their ruling number: they have three petals, three leaves, three sepals, a pistil with three carpels, and three stigmas. The flowering *Trillium* is purported to announce the return of migrating birds. Their scent, however, is not pleasant, but it attracts the flies that pollinate them. North American Indians use this plant to ease childbirth. The first pioneers learnt from them how to make use of its roots and the plant is still widely used in the treatment of illnesses suffered by women.

Opposite : Columbine or Granny's Bonnets *Aquilegia vulgaris*. Family : Ranunculaceae.

1 Lily of the Valley *Convallaria majalis*. Family : Liliaceae. **2** Solomon's Seal *Polygonatum vulgare*. Family : Liliaceae. **3** Cudweed *Gnaphalium silvaticum*. Family : Compositae. **4** Wood Avens *Geum silvaticum*. Family : Rosaceae. **5** Yellow Archangel *Lamium galeobdolon*. Family : Labiatae. **6** Celandine *Chelidonium majus*. Family : Papaveraceae.

Throughout history a number of strange and varied qualities have been attributed to celandine. It was widely used by the Greeks and Romans who believed that swallows used its nectar to cure their temporary attacks of blindness, which is why it is also known as swallow-wort. In the Middle Ages it was believed to possess magic powers. Alchemists used its nectar to help them in their eternal search for the philosopher's stone and it was later prescribed for the treatment of jaundice and liver complaints. Celandine was then abandoned during the Enlightenment and it didn't re-emerge as a medicinal ingredient until the twentieth century. Its active elements are similar to those of opium. It acts as a pain-killer and infusions from its leaves are antispasmodic and therefore recommended for angina and asthma. A decoction of its leaves or a little of its fresh juice diluted in plenty of water is still a popular remedy for ophthalmitis. The pure juice or freshly crushed roots are also reputed to eliminate corns and verrucas.

Opposite : Bergamot *Monarda didyma*. Family : Labiatae.

1 Nasturtium (tricolour) *Tropaeolum tricolorum*. Family : Tropaeolaceae. **2** *Arisaema sikokianum*. Family : Araceae. **3** *Roscoea purpurea*. Family : Zingiberaceae. **4** Flame Creeper *Tropaeolum speciosum*. Family : Tropaeolaceae. **5** *Nectaroscordum siculum*. Family : Liliaceae. **6** Pinesap *Monotropa hypopitys*. Family : Monotropaceae.

Because it lacks any chlorophyll, the pinesap lives on conifers. For a long time it was believed to be a just a saprophyte, but its vegetation system is much more complex. The pinesap lives in symbiosis with microscopic mushrooms, the filaments of which act as a bridge between the plant and the tree roots. These filaments transform the substances in the roots (particularly phosphates) into nutrients and carry them to the plant, while they in turn profit from the excess sugars it then releases. The pinesap harbours a large number of these mushrooms on its roots, along its stem and even in its flowers. Towards the end of the summer, its flower releases a delicate lemon scent and attracts insects. American Indians used the juice from its roots to make collyrium (eye-salve) while in Europe it was used to treat whooping cough.

Opposite : *Puschkinia scilloides*. Family : Liliaceae.

Mountain flowers

❋

The higher you climb, the more the different mountains around the world resemble each other. They are characterized by cold, snow, violent winds and intense light and the plants that manage to survive in these extreme conditions are rare. Mountain plants are generally small – it takes a lot of effort to grow against the wind. The fully-grown Arctic willow, for example, is only three centimetres high. To survive the cold, plants cluster together, cover themselves in a down coating, or transform their corollae into sun-traps in order to stay warm. These miniature solar ovens are a good source of heat: the difference between the outside and inside temperature of the flower is often more than 20°C (68°F)! And that's no secret to insects, who huddle inside the flower for the warmth. Long winters have forced many species to become annuals. Only once a year do they push up out of the soil, grow, flower, free their seeds, and die. Mountain flowers have a short life-span, but for the brief time they are in bloom, their colours are splendid. Their brightness and intensity are designed to attract the rare pollinators. Many of them are blue, the favorite colour of insects. The Himalayan poppy pictured opposite flowers at more than 5000 metres. The species that have learned to adapt to the rigorous conditions of the high mountains enjoy an abundance of space not found in the over-populated tropical forests and dense prairies. The higher you climb, the fewer the flowers. The tiny stitch-worts that grow at 6000 metres, have only lichens as neighbours.

Opposite: Himalayan Blue Poppy *Meconopsis baileyi.*
Family : Papaveraceae (Tibet–Nepal–Burma).

Right: Monkshood, *Aconitum napellus.*
Family : Ranunculaceae.

61

1 Spotted Gentian *Gentiana punctata*. Family : Gentianaceae (Europe). **2** Cross Gentian *Gentiana cruciata*. Family : Gentianaceae (Europe). **3** Fringed Gentian *Gentiana ciliata*. Family : Gentianaceae (Europe). **4** Stemless Gentian *Gentiana acaulis*. Family : Gentianaceae (Europe). **5** Great Yellow Gentian *Gentiana lutea*. Family : Gentianaceae (Europe). **6** Field Gentian *Gentiana campestris*. Family : Gentianaceae (Europe).

When the stemless gentian flower is blooming, its stamens develop before the stigma does. The anthers open, releasing pollen which falls to the base of the corolla, at which point the flower then closes tightly. Once the stigma is fully developed, the flower leans over and the pollen slides down onto the stigma, thus completing a perfect self-fertilization. Field gentian just bends its stamens rather than the whole flower and the stigma develops at the same time so that the pollen is deposited directly onto the female organs. These types of self-fertilizing or cleistogamous plants are very rare; in some cases certain plants will resort to this method when they have not been visited by pollinating insects.

Opposite : Spiked Rampion *Phyteuma spiicatum*. Family : Campanulaceae (Europe).

Following pages : Martagon Lily *Lilium martagon*. Family : Liliaceae (Europe).

1 Mourning Widow *Geranium phaeum*. Family : Geraniaceae (Europe). **2** Chives *Allium schoenoprasum*. Family : Liliaceae (Europe).
3 Alpine Aster *Aster alpinus*. Family : Compositae (Europe). **4** Mountain Clover *Trifolium alpestre*. Family : Leguminosae (Europe).
5 Pyrenean Squill *Scilla lilio-hyacinthus*. Family : Liliaceae (Europe). **6** Longspurred pansy *Viola calcarata*. Family : Violaceae (Europe).

Opposite : Edelweiss *Leontopodium alpinum*. Family : Compositae (Europe).

Edelweiss flowers alone are not attractive to insects, so they group together and the white woolly leaves surrounding them, disguised as petals, transform the whole inflorescence into a beautiful flower that resembles a white star. Edelweiss was once prized for its supposed medicinal properties; it was thought that it could cure rabies. More recently, however, it has been systematically torn from its natural habitat by visitors who rip the precious flowers up to take home as alpine souvenirs. Consequently it has become a very rare species, but thankfully picking edelweiss is now strictly forbidden.

1 Canary Bird *Trollius europaeus*. Family : Ranunculaceae (Europe). **2** Yellow Foxglove *Digitalis grandiflora*.
Family : Scrophulariaceae (Europe). **3** Brown Clover *Trifolium badium*. Family : Leguminosae (Europe). **4** Mountain Inula
Inula montana. Family : Compositae. **5** Round-leafed Wintergreen *Pyrola rotundifolia*. Family : Pyrolaceae (Europe).
6 St Bruno's Lily *Paradisia liliastrum*. Family : Liliaceae (Europe).

Opposite : Lady's Slipper Orchid *Cypripedium calceolus*. Family : Orchidaceae (Europe).

In early June, the lady's slipper orchid unfurls a beautiful flower that has a slipper-shaped labellum. The little scented brown spots at the
heart of the labellum attract bumble-bees. Once inside the slipper their only means of escape is by forcing their way through the opening
on the upper side where the reproductive organs are situated. This, the largest European orchid, is a rare species that can only be found in
some parts of the Alps, the Vosges and the Jura Mountains. The hitherto uncontrolled gathering of this wild orchid has led to the introduction of draconian protective measures. In some parts of Switzerland the flowers are systematically removed from the stems so that they
will not attract passers-by to pick them. Thanks to its rhizomes, the plant is able to propagate itself vegetatively. This is an extreme measure
but must be resorted to until man has learned to admire such rare and beautiful plants, without removing them from their natural habitat.

1 Knapweed *Centaurea uniflora*. Family : Compositae (Europe). **2** Alpine Thistle *Carlina acaulis*. Family : Compositae (Europe). When inclement weather threatens, the alpine thistle folds in its leaves to protect its flowers from the wind and rain. Shepherds once used this plant as a natural hygrometer: when they saw it closing they knew a storm was on its way and could shelter their flock in time. **3** *Allium ostrovskianum*. Family : Liliaceae (Asia). **4** Adenostyle Glabra *Adenostyles alpina*. Family : Compositae (Europe). **5** Marsh Orchid *Dactylorhiza incarnata*. Family : Orchidaceae (Europe). This orchid is now classified as a *Dactylorhiza* genus of which there are about twenty species. They are difficult to determine because they have a tendency to hybridize naturally. The marsh orchid prefers humid, even swampy conditions to alpine slopes. **6** Bilberry *Vaccinium myrtillus*. Family : Ericaeae (Europe).

Opposite : Musk Thistle *Carduus nutans*. Family : Compositae (Europe).

1 Alpine Anemone *Anemone alpina*. Family : Ranunculaceae (Europe). **2** Yellow Bellflower *Campanula thyrsoidea*. Family : Campanulaceae (Europe). **3** *Allium karataviense*. Family : Liliaceae (Asia). **4** Arnica *Arnica montana*. Family : Compositae (Europe). **5** Yellow Alpine Anemone *Anemone sulfurea*. Family : Ranunculaceae (Europe). **6** Wolf's Bane *Aconitum vulparia*. Family : Ranunculaceae (Europe).

The leaves, stems, flowers and above all the roots of *aconitum* contain alkaloids that include aconitine, the strongest narcotic produced by a plant. In general, the higher the plant grows the more dangerous it becomes. In the Middle Ages meat soaked in the juice extracted from aconite was used to trap foxes and wolves, hence the common name 'wolf's bane' and the latin name *vulparia* which means fox.

Opposite : Bearded Bellflower *Campanula barbata*. Family : Campanulaceae (Europe).

The bearded bellflower is an insect-loving plant. Its flowers secrete nectar which nourishes small bees. At nightfall and when it rains, its petals close sheltering the little insects nestling inside from the cold. There are many species of bellflower in the mountains that close their flowers in this way to protect their pollen from the dew and frost. The clustered bellflower even folds its leaves over the centre of its flower, covering it like a coat.

1 Yellow Melancholy Thistle *Cirsium erisithales*. Family : Compositae. **2** Pyrenean Star-of-Bethlehem *Ornithogalum pyrenaicum*. Family : Liliaceae. **3** Smooth Honeywort *Cerinthe glabra*. Family : Boraginaceae. **4** Lovage *Levisticum officinale*. Family : Umbelliferae. **5** Wood Anemone *Anemone nemorosa*. Family : Ranunculaceae. **6** Baldmoney *Meum athamanticum*. Family : Umbelliferae.

It is common knowledge among mountain shepherds that the fresh leaves of baldmoney are left untouched by their grazing livestock, but once dried the plant imbues hay with a delicate aroma and has a remarkably favourable effect on their milk production. Its roots are covered with tufts that have been likened to bear skin, hence another common name by which it is known, "bear root". In Switzerland, it is referred to as the "golden root" because an intensely perfumed essential oil can be extracted from its root.

Opposite : *Eucomis bicolor*. Family : Liliaceae (Drakensberg mountains, South Africa).

1 Large Masterwort *Astrantia major*. Family : Umbelliferae. **2** Herb Paris *Paris quadrifolia*. Family : Liliaceae. **3** Mountain Ash or Rowan *Sorbus aucuparia*. Family : Rosaceae. **4** Sweet Cicely *Myrrhis odorata*. Family : Umbelliferae. **5** Sneezewort *Achillea ptarmica*. Family : Compositae. **6** Pasque Flower *Anemone pulsatilla*. Family : Ranunculaceae.

Attached to its bended stem like a little bell, the *Anemone pulsatilla* (*anemo*s: "wind", *pulsare*: "to shake" or "flutter") sways back and forth in the wind. Like all other anemones, it is a poisonous plant. If its leaves are ingested they can cause serious burns in the mouth, followed by dizzy spells, convulsions and breathing difficulties. Nevertheless, the pasque flower is a stock item on any herbalist's inventory as, in very small doses, its extracts are known to have therapeutic properties. The diluted tincture is used by homeopaths in the treatment of anaemia, coryza, bronchitis, otitis, phlebitis, etc. In the sixteenth century, because of their similarity in appearance to a cloven hoof, the roots of the pasque flower were used in the making of ointments for illnesses supposedly inflicted by the devil, such as St Vitus' dance.

Opposite : Sea Holly *Eryngium bourgatii*. Family : Umbelliferae.

Flowers of the plains and prairies

✻

Plains and prairies in their truly natural state are rare. These great stretches of sun-drenched land and fertile soil came into existence following deforestation by man and the rise of agriculture. By acclimatizing species from every region of the world such as wheat, barley, corn, or potatoes, a new vegetal order was created. New flora began to develop next to these domesticated species, enjoying soils enriched with fertilizer and an ideal exposure to the sun, with no nearby trees to block the sun's rays. The only trees not cut down were the ones that could be exploited in some way.

In the fields, grasses pre-dominate. Most farmers regard them as troublesome "weeds", but they have learned to survive despite regular cuttings, tilling of the soil and the presence of chemical fertilizers. In their battle for survival alongside cultivated plants, many of these wild plants have adopted the tactic of mass invasion: 500,000 pimpernel seeds were counted (see page 78) on a surface area of just 100 square metres and each and every one of them retains its power of germination for several years! Meadows are often invaded by species of the Compositae family, which have evolved a "parachute" method to spread their seeds. Each seed is topped with small downy tufts that can carry it along on the wind for several miles. This system has proved to be a remarkably effective one as more than 10% of all the natural flowering plants belong to the Compositae family. Despite the valiant fight they put up, meadow flowers are nevertheless a threatened species. Today, pesticides have eliminated cornflowers and poppies from wheat fields, and the orchis and the ophrys have been killed off by overly-strong concentrations of fertilizers in the soil, while the corn-cockle has all but disappeared.

Opposite : Daisy *Bellis perennis.*
Family : Compositae.

Right : Tongue Orchid *Serapias lingua.*
Family : Orchidaceae.

1 Poppy *Papaver rhoeas*. Family : Papaveraceae. **2** Evening Primrose *Oenothera biennis*. Family : Oenotheraceae. **3** Tassel Grape Hyacinth *Muscari comosum*. Family : Liliaceae. **4** Corn-cockle *Lychnis githago*. Family : Caryophyllaceae. **5** Restharrow *Ononis repens*. Family : Leguminosae. **6** Scarlet Pimpernel *Anagallis arvensis*. Family : Primulaceae.

The scarlet pimpernel is often known as the "poor man's weather-glass". On bright, sunny mornings, the flowers open at eight o'clock; in cloudy weather they stay partially hidden beneath the leaves, and if there is rain in the air, they remain tightly closed.

Opposite : Eyebright *Euphrasia officinalis*. Family : Scrophulariaceae.

Despite having strong green leaves full of chlorophyll and capable of photosynthesis, the eyebright generally lives as a parasite on many various grasses and sedges – sometimes even on members of its own species. It was once claimed that eating eyebright could restore sight to the blind, but in reality its medicinal properties extend only as far as treating conjunctivitis.

1 Pyramidal Orchid *Anacamptis pyramidalis*. Family : Orchidaceae. **2** Bee Orchid *Ophrys apifera*. Family : Orchidaceae. **3** Spider Orchid *Ophrys sphegodes*. Family : Orchidaceae. **4** Fly Orchid *Ophrys muscifera*. Family : Orchidaceae. **5** Monkey Orchid *Orchis simia*. Family : Orchidaceae. **6** Woodcock Orchid *Ophrys scolopax*. Family : Orchidaceae.

Opposite : Military Orchid *Orchis militaris*. Family : Orchidaceae.

Wild orchids have two bulbs. Each year, a new tuber develops and feeds off the old one, enabling the plant to grow in a slightly different position, and therefore fresh soil, the following spring. Orchid bulbs are composed of a starch-like substance once used in Arab countries to prepare *salep*, a type of flour which, when mixed with hot water and honey, formed the basis of a highly nutritious drink.

Following pages : Greater Periwinkle *Vinca major*. Family : Apocynaceae.

The periwinkle is a symbol of humility and featured in various rituals of the Middle Ages, during which peasants would swear their allegiance to the lord of the manor by offering garlands made from the flowers. At Epiphany in France, periwinkle leaves were thrown into a fire and the future would be predicted according to the amount of noise produced by the plant as it burned.

1 Cape Leadwort *Plumbago capensis*. Family : Plumbaginaceae (South Africa). **2** *Combretum farinosum*. Family : Combretaceae (Zimbabwe). **3** *Clivia miniata*. Family : Amaryllidaceae (South Africa). **4** Bird of Paradise *Strelitzia reginae*. Family : Musaceae (South Africa). **5** *Chasmanthe floribunda*. Family : Iridaceae (South Africa). **6** *Agapanthus umbellatus*. Family : Liliaceae (South Africa).

With its strong, sweet perfume the sumptuous bird of paradise flower acts like a magnet to hummingbirds. As the bird forces its way through, the two petals open like a gateway to both the nectar and the stamens, which cover it with pollen as it drinks.

Opposite : African Hemp *Sparmannia africana*. Family : Tiliaceae (South Africa).

This shrub produces numerous stamens forming a red ball at the centre of the flower which barely have to be touched by an insect's feet or antennae for the tufts to open and reveal their pollen.

1 Double Soapwort *Saponaria officinalis*. Family : Caryophyllaceae. **2** Alstroemeria *Alstroemeria ligtu*. Family : Amaryllidaceae (Peru–Chile). **3** Great Mullein *Verbascum thapsus*. Family : Scrophulariaceae. **4** Peacock Flower *Tigridia pavonia*. Family : Iridaceae (Mexico). **5** Kidney Vetch *Anthyllis vulneraria*. Family : Leguminosae. **6** *Aphyllanthes monspeliensis*. Family : Liliaceae.

Rather than for the beauty of its flowers, the much hybridized alstroemeria was once prized for its tubers, which in Peru were cooked and eaten like potatoes.

Opposite : Pot Marigold *Calendula officinalis*. Family : Compositae.

The yellow flowers of the marigold were once considered to be effective in the treatment of jaundice. Interestingly, this is not at all far fetched as recent research has shown the flower to contain properties that can control the secretion of bile. The marigold was for a long time renowned as a magical talisman. It was thought that if you carried a marigold flower in your pocket while in court, you would be guaranteed clemency from the judge.

1 Cypress Spurge *Euphorbia cyparissias*. Family : Euphorbiaceae. **2** *Spiraea hypericifolia*. Family : Rosaceae. **3** Wormwood *Artemisia absinthium*. Family : Compositae. **4** Mignonette *Reseda odorata*. Family : Resedaceae. **5** Caraway *Carum carvi*. Family : Umbelliferae. **6** Yellow Bedstraw *Galium verum*. Family : Rubiaceae.

Opposite : Common Buckwheat *Polygonum fagopyrum*. Family : Polygonaceae.

Cattle that feed on buckwheat, either fresh or in their fodder, can often develop red blotches and irritable growths on their skin. The illness is known as fagopyrism and affects animals with a white or pied coat. Buckwheat contains a substance that becomes toxic and fluorescent when exposed to sunlight, and while the effect is not so strong as to turn the cattle into over-sized glow-worms, it nevertheless produces a strange glow beneath the white hide. Despite this toxic substance being concentrated in the flowers, bees remain unaffected, making a wonderful dark, rich and non-glowing honey from it.

Following pages : Marguerite, Moon Daisy *Leucanthemum vulgare*. Family : Compositae.

1 Salsify *Tragopogon porrifolius*. Family : Compositae. **2** Rock Rose *Helianthemum vulgare*. Family : Cistaceae. **3** Blue Cupidone *Catananche caerulea*. Family : Compositae. **4** Red Helleborine *Cephalanthera rubra*. Family : Orchidaceae. **5** Wild Mallow *Malva silvestris*. Family : Malvaceae. **6** *Acroclinum roseum*. Family : Compositae (Australia).

Opposite : Saffron Crocus *Crocus sativus*. Family : Iridaceae.

The characteristic orange-yellow powder of saffron is made neither from pollen nor the roots of an exotic plant, but from the stigma of a variety of crocus. By weight, saffron is the world's most expensive spice ($4500 per kilogram) and also one of the few grown on an industrial scale in Europe. France was once the major producing country. The flowers were harvested in September, in the morning before they had opened fully, with the stigmas then removed and laid out to dry on horsehair screens. It took 10 000 flowers to produce just 5 kilograms of stigmas, which in turn yielded a single kilogram of saffron after drying. Increasingly high labour costs led to the industry's disappearance in France, while Italy, Greece, Turkey and Kashmir have since become the main producers.

1 Borage *Borago officinalis*. Family : Boraginaceae. **2** Meadow Sage *Salvia pratensis*. Family : Labiatae.
3 Wild Carrot *Daucus carota*. Family : Umbelliferae. **4** Goat's Rue *Galega officinalis*. Family : Leguminosae.
5 Bulbous Corydalis *Corydalis bulbosa*. Family : Fumariaceae. **6** Herb Bennet *Geum urbanum*. Family : Rosaceae.

In Britain, priests would begin exorcism of a haunted place by fumigating with incense. They would then throw a herb bennet root onto a wood-burning stove and if the root burned normally, the place had been cleansed of the forces of evil. If, however, the root contorted, groaned and made squealing noises, that meant there were evil spirits still lurking!

Opposite : Deadnettle *Lamium album*. Family : Labiatae.

Following pages : Bleeding Heart *Dicentra spectabilis*. Family : Fumariaceae (Japan–China).

Geranium (eucalyptus-scented) *Pelargonium clorinda*. Family : Geraniaceae (South Africa).

Opposite : Geranium (rose-scented) *Pelargonium rosea*. Family : Geraniaceae (South Africa).

The island of Réunion in the Indian Ocean produces 100 metric tons of essential oil of rose per year. This essence, however, is extracted not from rose petals, but from the leaves of a geranium, *Pelargonium rosea*, which is a close relative of the familiar summer-flowering variety. This unusual plant was discovered in South Africa by the English, who brought it back to Europe in the seventeenth century. It gives off an intense fragrance at the slightest touch or when exposed to heat. In France, the leaves of these geraniums were first distilled almost a century later, and the plants began to be grown commercially in and around Grasse, later spreading to the rest of Provence, Corsica, Spain and ultimately Réunion, where they thrived remarkably. Today, France is the world's chief producer of essence of geranium, which is extracted on site using old-fashioned stills. Fields covering 7500 acres produce 120 000 metric tons of essential oil of rose. The geranium family appears to have a gift for impersonating other fragrances. Some smell of eucalyptus, others of lemon, mint, pine, balm, nutmeg, orange and even strawberry.

1 Cherry *Cerasus avium*. Family : Rosaceae. **2** Quince *Cydonia vulgaris*. Family : Rosaceae. **3** Apricot *Armeniaca vulgaris*. Family : Rosaceae. **4** Peach *Persica vulgaris*. Family : Rosaceae. **5** Common Pear *Pirus communis*. Family : Rosaceae. **6** Crab Apple *Malus communis*. Family : Rosaceae.

Fruit trees are an integral part of the rural landscape and their blossoming and fruiting have long given rise to a variety of superstitions, proverbs and legends. Peach blossom is, for example, a symbol of fickleness, as it falls at the first breath of wind. The ability to peel an apple and leave the skin in one piece was regarded as a way of predicting the future, and a young girl who could do this would supposedly be married within the year. Many proverbs about the cherry tree are linked to St George. "If it rains on St George's Day, only the donkeys will reap the benefits." (in other words, there will be no baskets of cherries for them to carry). A "plum eater" is a man whose betrothed marries another man. In days gone by, men who suffered such a fate would often find a plum tree branch lying at his door in mockery.

Opposite : Medlar *Mespilus germanica*. Family : Rosaceae.

1 Star of Bethlehem *Ornithogalum thyrsoides.* Family : Liliaceae. **2** Love-in-a-mist *Nigella damascena.* Family : Ranunculaceae. **3** Marsh Mallow *Althaea officinalis.* Family : Malvaceae. **4** Snowdrop *Galanthus nivalis.* Family : Amaryllidaceae. **5** Primrose Peerless *Narcissus tazetta.* Family : Amaryllidaceae. **6** Asphodel *Asphodelus albus.* Family : Liliaceae.

Opposite : Eleven o'clock Lady *Ornithogalum umbellatum.* Family : Liliaceae.

Like any conscientious naturalist, Linnaeus collected many plants and, being unable to study them all at once, kept them in vases. In doing so, he noticed that some flowers, even when removed from their natural habitat, continued to open at the same time each day as they do when growing in the ground. He deduced that many species have some sort of biological clock, which appeared to function independently of light, temperature and weather conditions. He thus established his "floral clock" theory, where each hour was marked by the opening or closing of a particular flower. At 3 am, bindweed was the first to open, followed by wild chicory, sow thistle and the water lily. At around 8 am, it was the turn of the marigold and chickweed, with the star of Bethlehem, or aptly named "eleven o'clock lady", opening its petals at 11 am. Early afternoon saw the ice plant and mouse ear close, then at 5 pm the marvel of Peru opened to attract moths. At about 8 pm, it was the turn of the night-flowering catchfly, then at midnight the queen of the night, both of which give off a rich scent.

1 Creeping Cinquefoil *Potentilla reptans*. Family : Rosaceae. **2** Virginian Witch Hazel *Hamamelis virginiana*. Family : Hamamelidaceae (United States–Canada). **3** Goat's Beard *Tragopogon pratensis*. Family : Compositae. **4** Crested Cow Wheat *Melampyrum cristatum*. Family : Scrophulariaceae. **5** Dandelion *Taraxacum officinale*. Family : Compositae. **6** Stinking Hellebore *Helleborus foetidus*. Family : Ranunculaceae.

Opposite : Giant Hemlock *Conium maculatum*. Family : Umbelliferae.

The medicinal and poisonous properties of hemlock have been known since Antiquity. The Greeks used it to make the poison that was administered to condemned political prisoners, and so it was that Socrates famously drank hemlock in 399 BC. All parts of the plant contain various extremely toxic alkaloids, but the unripe fruits are the most dangerous. Just six grams of fresh leaves can lead to death within three hours of ingestion. Hemlock acts in the same way as curare, paralyzing the muscles and diaphragm and destroying blood corpuscles. Strangely enough, hemlock has no ill effect on some animals. Starlings eat the seeds, while goats and sheep graze on the leaves.

106

1 Rough Marsh Mallow *Althaea hirsuta*. Family : Malvaceae. **2** Honesty *Lunaria annua*. Family : Cruciferae. **3** Red Clover *Trifolium rubens*. Family : Leguminosae. **4** Veronica *Veronica officinalis*. Family : Scrophulariaceae. **5** Herb Robert *Geranium robertianum*. Family : Geraniaceae. **6** Bugloss *Lycopsis arvensis*. Family : Boraginaceae.

Opposite : *Gladiolus segetum*. Family : Iridaceae.

1 *Collinsia heterophylla.* Family : Scrophulariaceae (California). **2** *Lobelia syphilitica.* Family : Campanulaceae (United States). The North American Indians made decoctions from lobelia roots with which they treated syphilis, and they used the smoked leaves to control asthma attacks. The various species of lobelia contain alkaloids like lobeline, which produce similar effects to nicotine. **3** *Tricyrtis hirta.* Family : Liliaceae (China–Japan). **4** Common Globularia *Globularia vulgaris.* Family : Globulariaceae. **5** *Phacelia tanacetifolia.* Family : Hydrophyllaceae (California). The flowers of this species are among the most alluring to bees. They will travel miles for its blue-mauve pollen and abundant nectar. Once considered nothing more than a weed, it is now widely cultivated by beekeepers. A couple of acres of *Phacelia* produces between five and six hundred kilograms of honey. **6** Peruvian Heliotrope *Heliotropum peruvianum.* Family : Boraginaceae.

Opposite : *Acidanthera bicolor.* Family : Iridaceae (Abyssinia).

Desert and scrubland flowers

✳

Unlike other habitats, deserts are defined mostly by what they lack: water, arable land and vegetation. A third of all land above sea-level is arid and every day the surface area covered by desertland increases by 25 000 acres. Any region that receives less than 25 centimetres of rainwater per year is considered a desert. Certain sections of the Sahara have not seen a drop of water in thirty years. The frozen lands of the Antarctic and the coasts of Chile, though shrouded in a permanent fog, also belong to this category. Though arid, these regions do not lack life. The plants have undergone numerous mutations to survive, the most common being the transformation of tissues into water reserves. They have become succulent. By the time it is 300 years old, the Arizona cereus is 20 metres high and can store over ten metric tons of water. To limit evaporation, its leaves have evolved into thin quills. Other species have pushed their roots deep down into the ground. In Australia, there is an orchid that grows completely underground, its flower included! Like mountain flowers, desert and scrubland flowers are often very beautiful but their lifespan is just as short. With activity reduced to a minimum during the day, the pollinators become active at night when white is the most visible colour. Scrubland flowers can tolerate the dryness, but they must also confront the wind, man and animals. The species that have adapted to this environment are sclerophyllus, which have tough leaves often covered in prickles. Scrubland is characterized by a wild mixture of small shrubs that give shelter to very perfumed flowers. Today these areas are under threat by the growing number of fires.

Opposite: *Trichocereus spachianus.* Family : Cactaceae (Argentina).

Right: Living Stones *Lithops sp.* Family : Aizoaceae (South Africa).

Following pages : *Crassula sp.* Family : Crassulaceae (South Africa).

1 *Mammillaria fraileana*. Family : Cactaceae (Mexico–California). **2** *Gymnocalycium horstii*. Family : Cactaceae (Brazil). **3** *Mila caespitosa*. Family : Cactaceae (Peru). The name of this genus of cactus is an anagram of Lima, the capital of Peru. **4** *Copiapoa longispina*. Family : Cactaceae (Chile). **5** *Matucana intertexta*. Family : Cactaceae (Peru). **6** *Ferocactus sinuatus*. Family : Cactaceae (Mexico).

Opposite : *Tephrocactus pentlandii*. Family : Cactaceae (Mexico).

1 *Lobivia pentlandii cristata*. Family : Cactaceae (Peru–Bolivia). **2** *Parodia tarabucensis*. Family : Cactaceae (Bolivia). **3** *Mammillaria occidentalis*. Family : Cactaceae (Mexico). **4** *Echinocereus reichenbachii*. Family : Cactaceae (United States–Mexico). **5** *Lobivia arachnacantha*. Family : Cactaceae (Bolivia). **6** *Lobivia emmae*. Family : Cactaceae (Bolivia).

Opposite : *Rebutia cintiensis*. Family : Cactaceae (Argentina).

Following pages : *Notocactus scopa*. Family : Cactaceae (Uruguay).

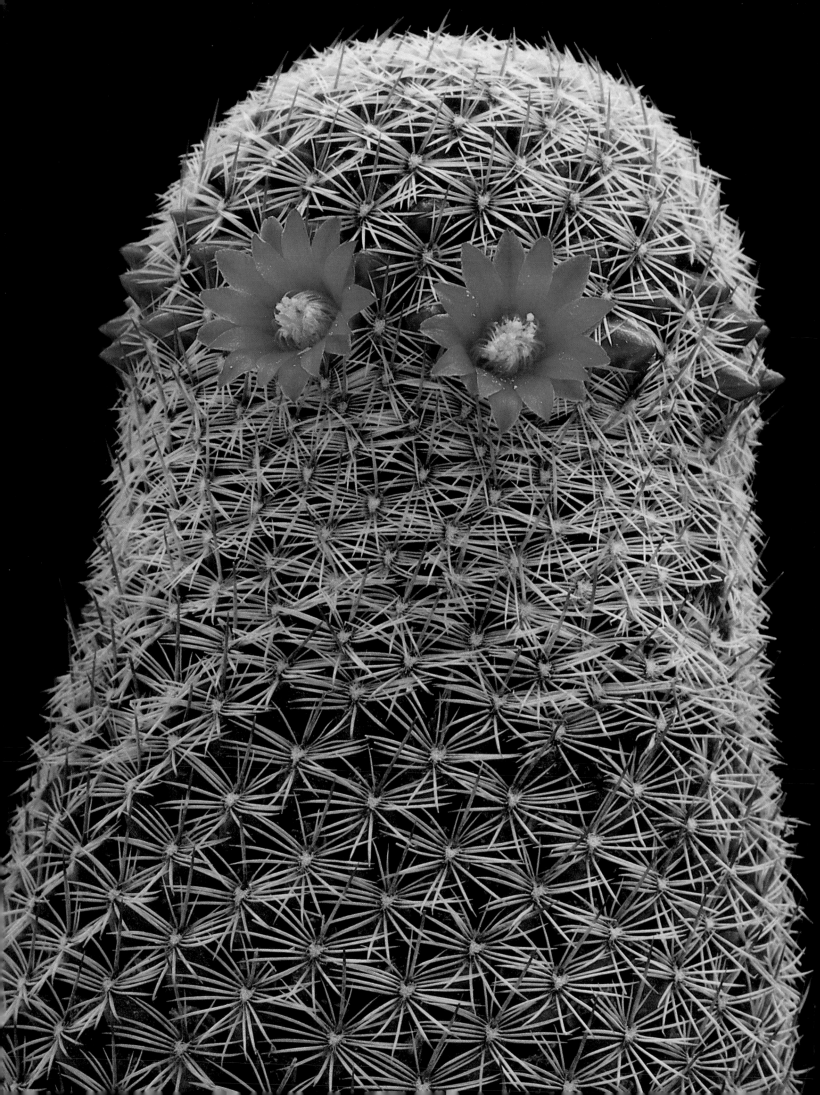

1 *Opuntia vestita*. Family : Cactaceae (Bolivia). 2 *Echinocereus pectinatus*. Family : Cactaceae (Arizona–Mexico). 3 *Chamaecereus silvestrii*. Family : Cactaceae (Argentina). 4 *Stenocactus multicostatus*. Family : Cactaceae (Mexico). 5 *Echinocereus roetteri*. Family : Cactaceae (Mexico). 6 *Mammillaria bombycina*. Family : Cactaceae (Mexico).

Opposite : *Mammillaria matudae*. Family : Cactaceae (Mexico).

1 *Kalanchoe pumila*. Family : Crassulaceae (Madagascar). **2** *Kalanchoe pinnata*. Family : Crassulaceae (Madagascar). **3** *Echeveria derembergii*. Family : Crassulaceae (Mexico). **4** *Kalanchoe fedtschenkoi*. Family : Crassulaceae (Madagascar). **5** *Kalanchoe sokotra*. Family : Crassulaceae (Madagascar). **6** Roof Houseleek *Sempervivum tectorum*. Family : Crassulaceae (Europe).

The paths that cut through the countryside of France are dotted with stone crosses, which are regularly tended and also covered with houseleek, one of the few succulents native to the country. Sheltering in the cracks between the stones, these plants feed from what little soil there is. They are left here because it is believed that they keep the devil away from these holy sites. It has been a common belief since Ancient times that it also keeps lightning at bay. In 812, Charlemagne ordered all buildings containing imperial treasures to be covered with houseleek. This tradition is still practised today in some rural areas, where it can often be seen growing on thatched roofs. According to one superstition, if you rub your hands with its juices, you can shoot through a red light without crashing!

Opposite : *Echeveria marnieri*. Family : Crassulaceae (Mexico).

Following pages : Rock Rose *Cistus albidus*. Family: Cistaceae

1 Indian Hemp *Cannabis indica*. Family : Cannabinaceae (India–Afghanistan). This is the plant that produces hashish.
2 Downy Thorn-apple *Datura metel*. Family : Solanaceae (Mexico). **3** Henbane *Hyoscyamus niger*. Family : Solanaceae (Europe).
In Shakespeare's Hamlet, the king of Denmark is poisoned by the sap of henbane poured into his ear while he is sleeping.
4 Downy Thorn-apple *Datura metel*. Family : Solanaceae (Mexico). **5** Peyote *Lophophora williamsii*. Family : Cactaceae (Mexico).
This plant produces mescaline, a substance similar to LSD. **6** Thorn-apple *Datura stramoine*. Family : Solanaceae (Europe).

With its frail blue-tinted petals, the poppy appears a harmless plant, but inside its fruit lies opium. This natural narcotic was widely used as a painkiller until the turn of the century when it soon became apparent how highly addictive it was. Its active ingredients are alkaloids which include morphine. Also a powerful sedative, opium was invaluable to surgeons at the time, but sadly it turned their patients into drug addicts. In the nineteenth century, a chemist called Dreser obtained a derivative of morphine which, when administered to addicts, enabled them to stop taking opium. This so-called miracle product was christened heroin, but its triumph was short-lived. Today we know all too well about its devastating effects.

Opposite : Opium Poppy *Papaver somniferum*. Family : Papaveraceae (Europe–The Orient).

Following pages : Jasmin officinal *Jasminum officinale*. Family : Oleaceae (India).

1 Coriander *Coriandrum sativum*. Family : Umbelliferae (Mediterranean coast). **2** Thyme *Thymus vulgaris*. Family : Labiatae (Mediterranean coast). **3** Sesame *Sesamum indicum*. Family : Pedalinaceae (Africa). **4** Rosemary *Rosmarinus officinalis*. Family : Labiatae (Mediterranean coast). **5** Basil *Ocinum basilicum*. Family : Labiatae (Southern Asia). **6** Dill *Anethum graveolens*. Family : Umbelliferae (Russia–Turkey).

Opposite : Cumin *Cuminum cyminum*. Family : Umbelliferae (Nile Valley).

133

1 Oleaster *Elaeagnus angustifolia*. Family : Elaeagnaceae (Southern Europe). **2** Chinese Persimmon *Diospyros kaki*. Family : Ebenaceae (China). Introduced to Europe in 1796 by the English botanist W. Roxburgh, this plant is cultivated for its edible fruit. **3** Pomegranate *Punica granatum*. Family : Punicaceae (Iran–Afghanistan). **4** Olive *Olea europaea*. Family : Oleaceae (Palestine–Syria–Greece). It is said that the olive tree only ever dies when it is killed by man. It can live up to two thousand years and for the Romans it was a symbol of peace and wisdom. The olive tree is practically the only plant whose oil comes from the flesh of its fruit (other vegetable oils are extracted from seeds). **5** Almond *Prunus amygdalus*. Family : Rosaceae (Afghanistan–Turkestan).The almond tree is the only *Prunus* with an edible seed. The wild species, however, grows very bitter and toxic varieties that contain the lethal poison, prussic acid. Yet this same species yields another variety of sweet almonds that are totally edible. Luckily, prussic acid is destroyed by heat, and so pastrycooks need not worry about using bitter almonds in the preparation of their confectionery. **6** Bay Tree *Laurus nobilis*. Family : Lauraceae (Mediterranean coast).

Opposite : Strawberry Tree *Arbutus unedo*. Family : Ericaceae (Mediterranean coast).

1 *Carduncellus monspeliensium.* Family : Compositae (France–Spain). **2** Carthamus *Kentrophyllum lanatum.* Family : Compositae (Mediterranean coast). **3** *Galactites tomentosa.* Family : Compositae (Mediterranean coast). **4** Safflower, Bastard Saffron *Carthamus tinctorius.* Family : Compositae (Mediterranean coast–Ethiopia). The flowers of this plant, once prized by painters for their red pigment, were also used to make imitation or "bastard" saffron. Its seeds produce a siccative oil used in the production of varnishes and soaps. **5** Blessed Thistle *Cnicus benedictus.* Family : Compositae (Mediterranean coast). During the Middle Ages, this plant was thought to possess such miraculous properties that it was believed to be blessed by God, hence the name. Its leaves can be used as a substitute for hops to make beer, which is why, during the First World War, when imports were blocked, it was widely cultivated in Germany. **6** *Asteriscus spinosus.* Family : Compositae (Mediterranean coast).

Opposite : Spanish Oyster Plant *Scolymus hispanicus.* Family : Compositae (Mediterranean coast–Madeira–Canary Islands).

1 Four o'clock Flower *Mirabilis jalapa*. Family : Nyctaginaceae (Peru). **2** Hottentots Fig *Carpobotrus acinaciformis*. Family : Aizoaceae (South Africa). **3** Clary *Salvia sclarea*. Family : Labiatae (Mediterranean coast). **4** Phlomis *Phlomis herba-venti*. Family : Labiatae (Mediterranean coast). **5** Oleander *Nerium oleander*. Family : Apocynaceae (Mediterranean coast). **6** Burning Bush *Dictamnus albus*. Family : Rutaceae (Mediterranean coast).

The flowers of the burning bush are filled with volatile essences and, on hot summer days, the air is heavy with their perfume. If you were to light a match by one of these plants these clouds of scented vapour would ignite, but the plant itself, though surrounded by blue flames, would remain intact. This delicate perfume is deceptive, however, as the burning bush is a toxic plant. Its roots contain an alkaloid called dictamine. In the Middle Ages, St Hildegarde harvested this plant and used it to make an ointment that was so strong that it could literally draw a broken arrow out of a wound.

Opposite : *Phoenocoma prolifera*. Family : Compositae (South Africa).

Aquatic flowers

✳

The planet's rivers, streams and marshes are packed with all kinds of organic matter which, when decomposed, is transformed into rich nutritive elements. The plants that survive the rising water levels, currents, and the climactic swings from drought to flooding, feed on these nutrients. Aquatic plants fall into two main categories. First of all, there are those which float. They have no system of attachment to the ground and draw their food directly from the water. These plants are very small and their flowers are not attractive enough to lure insects. Instead, they are pollinated by the wind. The second category has an effective root system that fixes them to the ground beneath the water. Because these plants are rooted in such an unstable substratum, they have evolved veined rhizomes that are long and creeping, with numerous roots that anchor them to the soil. These rhizomes also produce a number of different leaves on the same plant. This phenomenon is called heterophyllia and is a distinguishing feature of a number of aquatic plants. The sagittarius plant has three types of leaves. When submerged, they are ribbon-like and finely veined; when floating, they become elliptical; out of the water, they take on the shape of a spearhead (*sagitta* is the Latin word for arrow). Very gradually, the colonization of aquatic areas by plants alters the environment. As the plants develop, debris and soil accumulate around their roots. Fresh soil is created, and new species begin to grow. The water levels then drop and aquatic flowers disappear.

Opposite : White Water Lily *Nymphaea alba.* **Family :** Nymphaeaceae (Europe).

Left : *Mimulus spachianus.* **Family :** Scrophulariaceae.

141

1 Pickerel Weed *Pontederia cordata*. Family : Pontederiaceae (North America). **2** Grass of Parnassus *Parnassia palustris*. Family : Saxifragaceae. **3** Snowy Woodrush *Luzula nivea*. Family : Juncaceae. **4** Bulrush *Typha latifolia*. Family : Typhaceae. **5** Bogbean *Menyanthes trifoliata*. Family : Menyanthaceae. **6** American Arrowhead *Sagittaria latifolia*. Family : Alismataceae.

Opposite : Common Pitcher Plant *Sarracenia purpurea*. Family : Sarraceniaceae (Canada).

In the cold marshes of Canada, there is little nourishment to be had from the ground. Consequently, the pitcher plant has been forced to turn carnivore. Its leaves have evolved into scented pitchers at the bottom of which glistens a pool of enticing liquid. As soon as an insect lands on the leaf's edge it slips and falls into the liquid. The inside surface of the leaves is oily and lined with tiny hairs which point downwards forming an inescapable trap. The insect quickly drowns and is promptly digested by the plant. These pitcher traps do not kill all living things that visit them, however. Some flies lay their eggs on them, and some tiny frogs hang on their inside walls, snapping up the drowning insects before the plant has time to break them down.

1 Cat's Valerian *Valeriana officinalis*. Family : Valerianaceae. **2** Water Mint *Mentha aquatica*. Family : Labiatae.
3 *Cyperus alternifolius*. Family : Cyperaceae (Africa). **4** Wild Angelica *Angelica silvestris*. Family : Umbelliferae. **5** Touch-me-not
Impatiens noli tangere. Family : Balsaminaceae. **6** Meadowsweet *Filipendula ulmaria*. Family : Rosaceae.

During the Middle Ages, ponds, marshes and most areas of stagnant water carried malaria. It was thought then that the meadowsweet and willows, which grew vigorously in these humid conditions, had properties that could cure this disease and all the terrible fevers it brought with it. At the beginning of the nineteenth century the French scientist Leroux and the Swiss Pagenstecher succeeded in isolating first salicilin from the bark of the willow tree and then salicylic aldehyde from the flowers of meadowsweet. It didn't take long to discover that both these constituents had the same structure. Then in 1876, the chemist Hofmann synthesized acetylsalicylic acid and called it aspirin (a for acetyl and spir for spirea, another name for meadowsweet). With an average annual production of 80 billion tablets, aspirin is the world's most popular drug.

Opposite : Angelica *Angelica archangelica*. Family : Umbelliferae (Europe).

Following pages : Common Butterwort *Pinguicularia vulgaris*. Family : Lentibulariaceae.

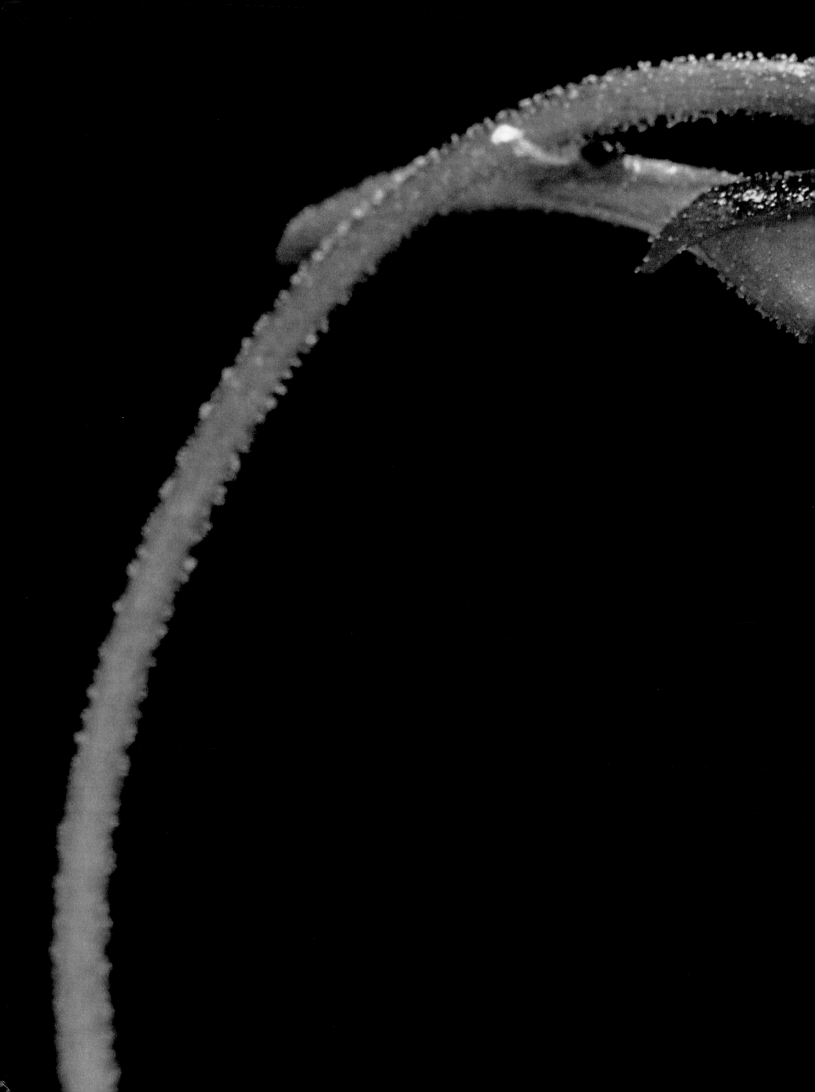

1 Butterwort *Pinguicularia moranensis*. Family : Lentibulariaceae (Mexico). **2** *Disa uniflora*. Family : Orchidaceae (South Africa). **3** *Canna coccinea*. Family : Cannaceae (India). **4** Snake's-head Fritillary *Fritillaria meleagris*. Family : Liliaceae. **5** *Cypella plumbea*. Family : Iridaceae (Argentina–Uruguay). **6** Lotus *Nelumbo nucifera*. Family : Nympheaceae (Subtropical Asia).

The lotus is, in many ways, an exceptional flower. It has an amazing 25-centimetre span and its petals are tough and waxy. The intensity of its perfume varies throughout the day. It is strongest at noon, after which time the petals begin to curl up slowly, and by sunset the flower is completely closed, emitting no scent at all. The lotus flower lives for only four days. The Japanese say that on the first day it resembles a Sake bottle, a Sake cup on the second, a soup bowl on the third and a saucer on the fourth. The fruit gradually develops into a strange upside-down cone shape that looks like the rose of a watering can. The top is flat and has twenty or so cells which contain seeds. When the fruit is ripe, it falls from its stalk and floats away face down in the water. Its covering slowly disintegrates and the seeds are released. As they are heavier than water, they sink and become embedded in the mud where they take root.

Opposite : *Zantedeschia rehmannii*. Family : Araceae (Transvaal).

149

1 Brooklime *Veronica beccabonga*. Family : Scrophulariaceae. **2** Marsh Thistle *Cirsium palustre*. Family : Compositae. **3** Water Avens *Geum rivale*. Family : Rosaceae. **4** *Mentha ceroina*. Family : Labiatae. **5** Bistort, Snake-root *Polygonum bistorta*. Family : Polygonaceae (Europe). **6** Skullcap *Scutellaria galericulata*. Family : Labiatae.

Opposite : Water Hyacinth *Eichhornia speciosa*. Family : Pontederiaceae.

At the Cotton Fair held in New Orleans in 1884, a new plant with blue flowers was presented for the first time on the Japanese stand to much acclaim. It was the water hyacinth. But no one could have guessed the ecological disaster this plant was to cause. Once placed in the lakes and ponds of Louisiana, the water hyacinth multiplied at a rapid rate and found its way into the bayou, rivers and all surrounding waterways. It wasn't long before everything was covered. The propellors of steamboats jammed and other aquatic plants perished, followed by fish and ducks who had nothing to feed on. Drastic measures were taken to combat this invasion – dynamite, fire, arsenic – but the hyacinths seemed invincible. This ongoing battle was costing so much that the plant soon got the nickname "Million-dollar-weed". In looking for ways to wipe it out, however, it was found to have some amazing properties. Scientists discovered that its tissues are capable of absorbing elements like cadmium, nickel or even mercury, which meant it could be turned to good use after all. It is now used to purify water and in India and the Philippines it is cultivated for its pulp which is combustible and gives methane.

150

1 Papyrus *Cyperus papyrus*. Family : Cyperaceae (Africa). **2** Elecampane *Inula helenium*. Family : Compositae. **3** Yellow Pimpernel *Lysimachia nummularia*. Family : Primulaceae. **4** Golden Club *Orontium aquaticum*. Family : Araceae (North America).
5 Mexican Water Lily *Nymphaea mexicana*. Family : Nympheaceae (Mexico). **6** Beardless Iris *Iris pseudacorus*. Family : Iridaceae.

The flowers of the Mexican water lily open only when the sun is out. Once fertilized, they grow a fruit that detaches itself when ripe and sinks. As it disintegrates the seeds inside are released. Because they are contained in little bubbles of air, they float to the surface and away from the mother plant. When the air bubble finally bursts, the seeds sink back down and settle into the mud where they germinate.

The fleur-de-lys, symbol of the French monarchy, is in fact an iris. It was first adopted by Clovis, king of the Francs. He was a pagan, but when faced with a troop of Germanic warriors he was afraid and promised to convert to Christianity if God came to his aid. The battle was won and Clovis kept his word; to mark the event, he replaced the three toads on his royal banner with three irises. The so-called beardless iris, which grows only in very shallow water, became a sacred symbol for the king, representing the shallow passage across the Rhine that God had shown him, where he chased off the invaders. This royal emblem was adopted by Louis VII during the Crusades and became known as the Fleur de Louis (flower of Louis) which was shortened to fleur-de-lys.

Opposite : *Caltha palustris*. Family : Ranunculaceae.

Coastal flowers

✻

Plants that survive in coastal and desert habitats share a lot in common. Like desert plants, the species that live by the sea are very robust – they have to be to survive on land that is often bare, arid and with constantly shifting soils. Botanists have classified them as Psammophytes, meaning plants that thrive in sand. To hold their own against the perpetual motion of the air and grains of sand, these species have developed tough leaves that are very small so that the surface of contact with the wind is kept to a minimum.

In general, coastal plants grow very close to the ground and put out plenty of roots that anchor them deeply in the soil and draw and store as much water as they can. The hardiest and most "fearless" of these plants are referred to by botanists as halophytes, meaning plants that love salt. Halophytes grow close to the sea so they are in constant contact with salt water which laps around them or else they are completely submerged by tides. Salt is the mortal enemy of most plants, but halophytes are adapted to survive these conditions. Their stems are fleshy and the waxy or hairy epidermis protects them from rapid evaporation. Added to this, their cytoplasmic juices have a high salt content which gives them a higher osmotic pressure than other plants, so they are able to absorb salt water. For most other vegetation, this terrain is physiologically too dry, but these pioneering plants gradually stabilize the soil and as the conditions become more habitable, so other plants move in and grow. But, as in aquatic environments, when confronted by new invaders, the colonizers are eventually forced to retreat and return to the sand, salt and wind.

Opposite : Sea Holly
Eryngium maritimum. Family : Umbelliferae.

Right : *Canarina canariensis.*
Family : Campanulaceae (Canary Islands).

155

1 Yellow Mignonette *Reseda lutea*. Family : Resedaceae. **2** Birthwort *Aristolochia clematitis*. Family : Aristolochiaceae. **3** *Abronia latifolia*. Family : Nyctaginaceae (California). **4** Yellow Sternbergia *Sternbergia lutea*. Family : Amaryllidaceae. **5** Broom *Sarothamnus scoparius*. Family : Leguminosae. **6** Solidago or Golden Rod *Solidago virga-aurea*. Family : Compositae.

Opposite : Gorse *Ulex europaeus*. Family : Leguminosae.

The fact that gorse flowers all year round has made it the sworn enemy of the devil. According to a Scottish legend, Satan had become so despondent at seeing nobody entering Hell that he appealed to God, who promised him the souls of all those who died while the moorland was not in bloom. A delighted Satan returned to Earth, but the months passed and flowers still covered the gorse bushes. In a fit of frustration, he sowed the ground with barley and, by converting it into malt, invented whisky. He built pubs along the road leading to Heaven where the Scots would stop first for one dram, then another – when they left, totally inebriated, he would escort them to Hell. Scottish houses and fields are often surrounded with gorse so as to protect against evil curses.

1 Sand Everlasting *Helichrysum staechas*. Family : Compositae. **2** Lousebur *Xanthium strumarium*.
Family : Ambrosiaceae. **3** Ragwort *Senecio cineraria*. Family : Compositae. **4** Hare's Ear *Buplevrum fruticosum*.
Family : Umbelliferae. **5** Yellow Asphodel *Asphodeline lutea*. Family : Liliaceae (Mediterranean coast). **6** Cotton Lavender
Santolina chamaecyparissus. Family : Compositae. Its flowering shoots are used as an insecticide against clothes moths.

Opposite : Tree Mallow *Lavatera arborea*. Family : Malvaceae.

1 Sea Rocket *Cakile maritima*. Family : Cruciferae. **2** Sea Daffodil, Sea Lily *Pancratium maritimum*. Family : Amaryllidaceae (Mediterranean coast). All species have bulbs containing a neurotoxin which North African witch doctors would rub into cuts made in the scalp to provoke hallucinations. The species that grows along the Mediterranean coast is under threat of extinction owing to the numbers of tourists using the beaches. **3** Tamarisk *Tamarix parviflora*. Family : Tamaricaceae. **4** Acanthus or Bear's Breeches *Acanthus mollis*. Family : Acanthaceae. The leaves of this species are often credited as the model for the design on the capitals of Corinthian columns. This acanthus, however, grows wild only in northern Greece and could therefore not have been used by the Corinthians. Exact reproductions of the *Acanthus mollis* leaves are found only on Macedonian gold produced during the 4th century BC. **5** Sea Cudweed *Diotis maritima*. Family : Compositae. **6** Sea Lavender *Limonium tartaricum*. Family : Plumbaginaceae.

Opposite : Thrift *Armeria maritima*. Family : Plumbaginaceae.

Following pages : Protea *Protea spachianus* Family : Proteaceae (South Africa).

1 Laurel-leaved Protea *Protea laurifolia*. Family : Proteaceae (South Africa). **2** Proliferous Pink *Dianthus prolifer*. Family : Caryophyllaceae. **3** Stock *Matthiola sinuata*. Family : Cruciferae. **4** *Leucospermum nutans*. Family : Proteaceae (South Africa). **5** Dragon Arum *Arum dracunculus*. Family : Araceae (Mediterranean coast of France) **6** Spurge Flax *Daphne gnidium*. Family : Thymelaeaceae.

Opposite : Giant Protea *Protea cynaroides*. Family : Proteaceae (the national flower of South Africa)

Proteus, the Greek god of stormy seas, was blessed with the ability to change his shape at will. The aptly-named protea family comprises over a thousand species, mimicking perfectly other plants to which they are often botanically unrelated - some proteas masquerade as marguerites, others as ginger, pine cones, laurel or even, in the case of the giant protea, artichokes. The flowers in themselves are nothing out of the ordinary, but when they occur in inflorescences measuring 30 centimetres across, they provide a magnificent spectacle. They are brightly coloured and have a solid structure to support their often heavy pollinators – marsupials, mice and birds – which draw the nectar from the thousand or so flowers in each inflorescence. This nectar is so sweet that it is also harvested to make cordials.

1 Vincetoxicum *Vincetoxicum officinale*. Family : Asclepiadaceae. Vincetoxicum was once used to treat the plague and snakebites.
2 *Echinophora spinosa*. Family : Umbelliferae (Rhone Delta, Mediterranean coast). The root is eaten in the Far East.
3 Nodding Catchfly *Silene nutans*. Family : Caryophyllaceae. The petals of this species close up when the heat becomes
too strong. Along with grains of sand, minute insects are caught on its sticky stems, hence its common name.
4 *Carex spachianus* Family : Cyperaceae. **5** Shepherd Cress *Teesdalia nudicaulis*. Family : Cruciferae.
6 Ice Plant *Mesembryanthemum crystallinum*. Family : Mesembryanthemaceae (Mediterranean coast). The leaves,
which look like they are permanently covered with dew, are edible and have a very refreshing and slightly tart flavour.

Opposite : Sea Squill, Sea Onion *Urginea maritima*. Family : Liliaceae (Greece).

The huge bulb of the sea squill, which can often grow to the size of a child's head, has been a symbol of strength since Antiquity,
and Greek islanders hang it over their doors as an amulet against evil spirits. The squill was also used against rodent infestation –
its bulbs contain a scillaglucoside that is highly poisonous to rats.

Man-made hybrids

Five thousand years ago, the Chinese were already selectively breeding wild roses to produce new varieties. Such was the fashion for rose gardens under the Han dynasty that they encroached on land needed for agriculture and the emperor was forced to order the destruction of some gardens and limit the cultivation of the flowers. During the same period, rose growing flourished in Egypt and Rome. Roses, like many other flowers, were transformed by cross-pollination and the five petals of the wild varieties replaced by over one hundred in modern hybrids, while more abundantly flowering specimens were developed, along with new shapes and colours. This kind of manipulation was always carried out within the same genus. Varieties of lily, rose or iris were interbred and the process repeated on the new creations. With the rise of genetics, horticulturists are now able to produce new flowers by cross-pollinating different genuses – the equivalent of crossing a horse with a chicken! The first successful results came with orchids, flowers that had long resisted domestication. Thus, the *Vandaenopsis* is a man-made cross between the *Vanda* and the *Phalaenopsis*, and the *Brassolaeliocattleya* a hybrid of the *Brassia*, the *Laelia* and the *Cattleya*. Research into new plants is geared towards the consumer: lilies without stamens have been developed to avoid pollen stains; a chestnut with sterile flowers has been bred so that its fruits do not fall on main roads, and so on.

Although anything seems possible, after thousands of years spent attempting to remodel nature, man has still not managed to create a truly black flower, a blue rose or a red iris.

Opposite : Amaryllis 'Picotée' *Hippeastrum* ×. Family : Amaryllidaceae.

Right : Rose *Rosa* ×. Family : Rosaceae.

1 Rose 'de Puteaux' *Rosa* ×. Family : Rosaceae. This rose was brought back from the Crusades and was cultivated during the 19th century in Puteaux in France to provide petals for drying. **2** Rose 'Mermaid' *Rosa* ×. Family : Rosaceae. Created in 1918. **3** Rose 'Veilchenblau' *Rosa* ×. Family : Rosaceae. Produced in 1909. The old-fashioned charm of the flowers is combined with an unusual scent of apples which emanates from the leaves. **4** Rose 'Parfum de L'Haÿ' *Rosa* ×. Family : Rosaceae. Produced in 1901. **5** Rose 'Ghislaine de Féligonde' *Rosa* ×. Family : Rosaceae. Produced in 1916, this rose is grown in old established gardens in northern France. **6** Rose 'Honorine de Brabant' *Rosa* ×. Family : Rosaceae. Produced in 1916, this is one of the rare old roses that flower constantly throughout the summer.

Opposite : Rose 'Louise Odier' *Rosa* ×. Family : Rosaceae. Produced in 1851. The flowers of this variety, along with those of the "Queen Victoria", are characterized as "perfect roses".

The thousands of roses bred from the 250 or so wild species are classified into one of two categories – old roses and modern roses. Old roses can strictly be referred to as such only if they were created before 1920 and are deciduous. Although their flowering season is rather short (May–June), they have an exquisite perfume.

Following pages : Hedgehog Rose *Rosa rugosa* ×. Family : Rosaceae.

1 Rose 'Pierre de Ronsard' *Rosa* ×. Family : Rosaceae. Created in 1986 **2** Rose 'Handel' *Rosa* ×. Family : Rosaceae. A climbing rose produced in 1965 by McGredy. **3** Rose 'Souvenir du Dr Jamain' *Rosa* ×. Family : Rosaceae. This rose was created well before 1920, but is often classed with modern roses because of its remontant flowering habit. **4** Rose 'Golden wing' *Rosa* ×. Family : Rosaceae. An almost perpetual-flowering rose, created in 1956. Its flowers have a delicate perfume rare among modern roses. **5** Rose 'Queen Elizabeth' *Rosa* ×. Family : Rosaceae. The most famous of the floribunda roses, created in 1955. **6** Rose 'Hannah Gordon' *Rosa* ×. Family : Rosaceae. Floribunda created in 1983.

Opposite : Rose 'Westerland' *Rosa* ×. Family : Rosaceae. Rosa floribunda produced in 1969.

In the years following the Second World War there was a renewed interest in rose breeding: the new floribunda roses brought plants bearing clusters of flowers; the new hybrid tea varieties produced large flowers in increasingly varied colours, particularly bright yellow; and the number of remontant roses increased ("remontant" meaning that they flower more than once during the season). Modern roses flower continually from May to October.

1 Iris 'Gay Parasol' *Iris* ×. Family : Iridaceae. **2** Iris 'Temple Gold' *Iris* ×. Family : Iridaceae. **3** Iris 'Marilyn Holloway' *Iris* ×. Family : Iridaceae. **4** Iris *Iris xiphium* ×. Family : Iridaceae. **5** Iris 'Aril Lady' *Iris* ×. Family : Iridaceae. **6** Iris 'Speckless' *Iris* ×. Family : Iridaceae.

Opposite : Iris 'Storm Center' (mother) *Iris* × + Iris 'Victoria falls' (father) *Iris* × = Iris 'Duranus' (hybrid) *Iris* ×. Family : Iridaceae.

The *Iris* genus comprises over 300 species of perennial with rhizomatous, bulbous or fleshy rooted plants from which an infinite number of varieties have been produced. The finest specimens come from North America and France. It can take between eight and ten years from the moment when the pollen from one flower is placed on the stigma of another to the marketing of a new hybrid. Only three or four out of over 1000 experimental hybrids will make it into the catalogue. Breeders still dream of achieving their ideal – the production of a red iris.

Following pages : Common Iris *Iris* ×. Family : Iridaceae.

1 Clematis 'Ville de Lyon' *Clematis* ×. Family : Ranunculaceae. This hybrid of *Clematis viticella* was created in 1899 by Francisque Morel, a grower in Lyon. **2** Clematis 'Rouge Cardinal' *Clematis* ×. Family : Ranunculaceae. **3** Clematis 'Jackmanii' *Clematis* ×. Family : Ranunculaceae. This hybrid, created by Jackmann in 1860, has produced many mauve or pink varieties. **4** *Clematis montana* ×. Family : Ranunculaceae. The wild species is a tall-growing liana, native to the Himalayas, and has produced many white or pale blue varieties.

Opposite : Clematis 'Nelly Moser' *Clematis* ×. Family : Ranunculaceae. This clematis, produced in 1898, is a hybrid of *Clematis lanuginosa* and *Clematis patens*.

Although the flowers of the clematis, traveller's joy (see page 42) are too small to make it an ornamental plant, the introduction of clematis from China, Portugal, the Caucasus, Iran and North America, and the subsequent hybridization of these species, has led to the cultivation of the plant in parks and gardens.

1 Tuberous Begonia *Begonia tuberhybrida*. Family : Begoniaceae. **2** Begonia *Begonia fimbriata*. Family : Begoniaceae. **3** Begonia *Begonia pendulata*. Family : Begoniaceae. **4** Begonia 'Gloire de Lorraine' *Begonia tuberhybrida*. Family : Begoniaceae. **5** Begonia *Begonia crispa marginata*. Family : Begoniaceae. **6** Tuberous begonia *Begonia tuberhybrida*. Family : Begoniaceae.

Opposite : Double-flowered Tuberous Begonia *Begonia tuberhybrida*. Family : Begoniaceae.

In 1687, King Louis XIV of France ordered Michel Bégon, master of the galleys at Marseille, to find a naturalist who would take part in a scientific voyage to America, organized for the purpose of bringing back medicinal plants. A Franciscan monk called Charles Plumier was chosen, and during the two year voyage he collected hundreds of previously unknown species. In a forest in the Dominican Republic, he discovered a plant with asymmetrical leaves which he named begonia – in honour of his benefactor's wife, whom he secretly loved. Many years later in 1856, the begonia rex, with its remarkable brown and silvery foliage, was discovered in the jungles of Assam and, later still, tuberous begonias in the mountains of Bolivia and Peru. Horticulturists crossed all these new species and today there are thousands of varieties, the most famous hybrids being developed in Belgium.

1 Coreopsis *Coreopsis grandiflora*. Family : Compositae. **2** Cosmos *Cosmos bipinnatus*. Family : Compositae. **3** *Dimorphotheca aurantiaca*. Family : Compositae. **4** Gerbera *Gerbera jamesonii*. Family : Compositae. **5** Cosmos *Cosmos bipinnatus*. Family : Compositae. **6** Cosmos *Cosmos bipinnatus*. Family : Compositae.

Opposite : Gerbera *Gerbera jamesonii*. Family : Compositae.

1 Frilly Oriental Poppy *Papaver orientale* ×. Family : Papaveraceae. **2** Gerbera *Gerbera* ×. Family : Compositae. **3** Persian Buttercup *Renunculus asiaticus.* Family : Ranunculaceae. **4** "De Caen" Anemone *Anemone* ×. Family : Ranunculaceae. *Anemone coronaria* has produced many varieties, known as florists' or "de Caen" anemones. **5** Persian Buttercup *Renunculus asiaticus.* Family : Ranunculaceae. **6** Dahlia *Dahlia* ×. Family : Compositae.

Dahlias are native to Mexico and South America and were originally introduced to Europe for their edible roots. Their tubers, however, have an overly bitter taste and the plants would have been quickly forgotten were it not for the fact that their magnificent red flowers made them so attractive to gardeners. The wild species have today been replaced by hybrids, and dahlia flowers display a wonderful array of colours (except blue). They are classified by shape into five major categories: single-flowered; double-flowered; pompom or small-flowered; dwarf; and cactus.

Opposite : Poppy 'Exotica' *Papaver orientale* × . Family : Papaveraceae.

1 Darwin Tulip *Tulipa* ×. Family : Liliaceae. **2** Lily-flowered tulip *Tulipa* ×. Family : Liliaceae. **3** Parrot Tulip *Tulipa* ×.
Family : Liliaceae. **4** Parrot Tulip *Tulipa* ×. Family : Liliaceae. **5** Rembrandt Tulip *Tulipa* ×. Family : Liliaceae.
6 *Tulipa* ×. Family : Liliaceae.

Opposite : Rembrandt Tulip *Tulipa* × . Family : Liliaceae.

Tulips were the root cause of a crisis that gripped western Europe in the early seventeenth century. The tulip craze began when the
Austrian emperor Ferdinand I planted his garden with a few bulbs that had been brought back from Constantinople by one of his
ambassadors. Ferdinand's tulips were stolen and subsequently appeared in Holland. Apart from the fact that they were very rare, what
made these flowers so special was their ability to change colour and shape naturally. These spontaneous mutations remained a mystery
for a long time, but they are now known to be caused by a virus that alters the genetic composition of the cells controlling inherited
colour. These unusual mutating flowers became highly sought after and their market price soared, with three *Semper Augustus* bulbs
being sold for the equivalent today of $24 000. In 1637, however, the government banned such financial speculation, and as growers
created stable varieties, tulips began to be cultivated on an industrial scale and the market collapsed.

Following pages : Crinum *Crinum* ×. Family : Amaryllidaceae.

1 Fuchsia *Fuchsia* ×. Family : Onagraceae. **2** Russell Lupin *Lupinus polyphyllus*. Family : Leguminosae. **3** Gladiolus *Gladiolus* ×. Family : Iridaceae. **4** Hyacinth *Hyacinthus orientalis*. Family : Liliaceae. **5** Foxglove *Digitalis* ×. Family : Scrophulariaceae. **6** Single-flowered Chrysanthemum *Chrysanthemum* ×. Family : Compositae.

Opposite : Gladiolus *Gladiolus* ×. Family : Iridaceae.

The Chinese have been growing chrysanthemums for over two thousand years and horticulturists have now created several thousand hybrids from the 200 or so wild species in an array of different shapes and colours. In France, the chrysanthemum is associated with All Souls' Day and its cultivation is carefully scheduled so that it flowers by November 1. As a bud requires a regular nine and a half hours of darkness in order to develop, the flowering process is triggered when the nights begin to draw in. While this process can be slowed down by illumination at night, it can also be accelerated by covering the plants with black plastic. By using extremely precise manipulation techniques, professional growers can make the plants flower whenever they wish. As the saying goes, "chrysanthemum-growing is to horticulture what body-building is to sport". In China and Korea, the chrysanthemum is associated with births and marriages. It is the fourth noble plant after the ornamental cherry, bamboo and the orchid, and has a great fascination for oriental gardeners.

Following pages : Petunia *Petunia* ×. Family : Solanaceae.

1 Shooting Stars *Dodecatheon* ×. Family : Primulaceae. **2** Common Snapdragon *Antirrhinum majus*. Family : Scrophulariaceae. **3** Freesia *Freesia* ×. Family : Iridaceae. **4** China Aster *Callistephus chinensis*. Family : Compositae. **5** Sweet Pea *Lathyrus odoratus*. Family : Leguminosae. **6** Camellia 'Gay Time' *Camellia japonica* ×. Family : Theaceae.

The camellia first arrived in Europe as the result of a deception. The Chinese were anxious to retain their tea-growing monopoly and sold botanists young camellia shoots that bore a confusing resemblance to the tea plants that they were looking for. The two plants belong to the same family and their foliage is almost identical, the only difference being in the flowers – while those of the tea plant are white, those of the original species of camellia are red. This fake tea plant was to be made famous in the nineteenth century by Marie Duplessis, immortalized by Alexandre Dumas Fils as Marguerite Gautier in *La Dame aux Camélias*.

Opposite : Giant Allium *Allium giganteum*. Family : Liliaceae.

1 Pelargonium *Pelargonium × domesticum*. Family : Geraniaceae. **2** Pelargonium *Pelargonium × domesticum*. Family : Geraniaceae.
3 Pelargonium *Pelargonium × domesticum*. Family : Geraniaceae. **4** Pelargonium *Pelargonium × domesticum*.
Family : Geraniaceae. **5** Pelargonium *Pelargonium × domesticum*. Family : Geraniaceae.
6 Pelargonium 'Crocodile' *Pelargonium × domesticum*. Family : Geraniaceae.

Opposite : Pelargonium 'Beauty of Gold' *Pelargonium × domesticum*. Family : Geraniaceae.

The geraniums that are such a familiar sight on Mediterranean balconies are hybrids developed from the pelargonium species native to South Africa (see pages 100-101), annual plants that are killed off by the first frosts. Owing to the fact that they flower from seed in a year, are tolerant of direct sunlight and require very little attention, they have become extremely popular. True geraniums are perennials and many species, such as the black geranium, are part of the native flora of Europe (see page 67).

1 Aquilegia *Aquilegia* ×. Family : Ranunculaceae. **2** Purple Rudbeckia *Rudbeckia purpurea*. Family : Compositae. **3** Dahlia *Dahlia* ×
Family : Compositae. **4** Blanketflower *Gaillardia* ×. Family : Compositae. **5** Everlasting Flower *Helichrysum bracteatum*.
Family : Compositae. Many varieties used for bouquets of dried flowers have been produced from the wild species, which is native to
Australia. **6** Chrysanthemum *Chrysanthemum* ×. Family : Compositae.

Opposite : Sunflower *Helianthus* ×. Family : Compositae. Although farmers in Kansas regard the sunflower as a weed,
elsewhere its many varieties are highly valued as large ornamental flowers.

1 Pansy *Viola wittrockiana* ×. Family : Violaceae. **2** Common Primrose *Primula* ×. Family : Primulaceae. **3** Pansy *Viola wittrockiana* ×. Family : Violaceae. **4** Common Primrose *Primula* ×. Family : Primulaceae. **5** Pansy *Viola wittrockiana* ×. Family : Violaceae. **6** Common Primrose *Primula* ×. Family : Primulaceae.

Opposite : Narcissus 'Golden Harvest' *Narcissus* ×. Family : Amaryllidaceae. Narcissus 'Ice Follies' *Narcissus* ×. Family : Amaryllidaceae. Narcissus 'Professor Einstein' *Narcissus* ×. Family : Amaryllidaceae.

Narcissi are among the most popular spring flowers. Thousands of hybrid varieties have been produced from the 60 known wild species and are classified according to flower shape, such as large and small corona narcissi, butterfly-flowered narcissi and trumpet narcissi. Various techniques are used to alter the flowering season – it can be brought forward by keeping the bulbs in cold storage throughout the summer to simulate winter, or delayed by storing them at a warm and constant temperature. The Dutch have a practical monopoly in the development of new varieties and are the largest bulb producers.

Following pages : Rhododendron 'Nova Zemblack' *Rhododendron* ×. Family : Ericaceae.

1 Lily 'Mabel Violet' *Lilium* ×. Family : Liliaceae. **2** Lily 'Apple Blossom' *Lilium* ×. Family : Liliaceae. **3** Tiger Lily *Lilium tigrinum*. Family : Liliaceae. **4** Regal Lily *Lilium regale*. Family : Liliaceae. **5** Lily 'Casablanca' *Lilium* ×. Family : Liliaceae. **6** Lily *Lilium* ×. Family : Liliaceae.

Opposite : Lily 'African Queen' *Lilium* ×. Family : Liliaceae.

According to legend, after she had been deceived into suckling Hercules, a drop of milk fell from Juno's breast and from it sprang a lily. Venus later became jealous of the flower's purity of colour and placed long yellow stamens in its white calyx which would leave indelible pollen stains if touched. The cross-pollination of species from Asia – China in the case of the regal lily, Korea in the case of the tiger lily – has today yielded flowers of every colour and even some that have no pollen.

1 Carnation *Dianthus caryophyllus*. Family : Caryophyllaceae. **2** Carnation *Dianthus caryophyllus*. Family : Caryophyllaceae. **3** Indian Pink *Dianthus chinensis*. Family : Caryophyllaceae. **4** Carnation *Dianthus caryophyllus*. Family : Caryophyllaceae. **5** Indian Pink *Dianthus chinensis*. Family : Caryophyllaceae. **6** Sweet William *Dianthus barbatus*. Family : Caryophyllaceae.

Opposite : Sweet William *Dianthus barbatus*. Family : Caryophyllaceae.

In Spain, the carnation is the symbol of women from Andalucia. During fiesta time, flamenco dancers wear a red carnation in their chignons and brightly coloured dresses which supposedly represent the flower's corolla. It is worn behind the ear to a bullfight – the left ear if the girl is single, the right if she is spoken for – and when the bull is killed, fans throw bouquets of red carnations to the brave toreador in the ring. The Italians traditionally associate white carnations with the evil eye, while in Brazil the flower is known as the "coffin nail" and is never used in a bouquet. Despite these superstitions, the carnation is the most widely sold flower in the world alongside the rose, its largest producers being Poland, France and Colombia.

1 Lisianthus *Lisianthus russellianus*. Family : Gentianaceae. **2** China Aster *Callistephus chinensis*. Family : Compositae. **3** Verbena *Verbena* ×. Family : Verbenaceae. **4** Feather Grape Hyacinth *Muscari comosum plumosum*. Family : Liliaceae. **5** Delphinium *Delphinium* ×. Family : Ranunculaceae. **6** Hydrangea *Hydrangea macrophylla*. Family : Saxifragaceae.

Opposite : Imperial Peony *Paeonia lactiflora*. Family : Ranunculaceae.

The peony has always been regarded as a health-giving plant and many varieties have been developed from the wild species native to Mongolia. In Europe and Asia alike, its seeds were thought to soothe epileptic fits and other convulsive attacks. It was also believed that its leaves acted as a contraceptive, and young girls attending a ball with an over-amorous suitor often wore them in their shoes or stockings!

1 *Laeliocattleya* 'Consul'. Family : Orchidaceae. **2** *Cattleya* 'Pontcoarl'. Family : Orchidaceae.

Opposite : *Brassolaeliocattleya* 'Parador × Harlequin'. Family : Orchidaceae.

William Cattley, the great collector of exotic flowers, was regularly sent plants from South America and, in 1818, a parcel arrived from Brazil which had been wrapped in thick leaves for protection. He potted up his new specimens and left the plant wrapping in a corner of his greenhouse. Some months later, the wrapping produced glorious mauve flowers with purple markings. Astonished by his discovery, Cattley immediately contacted the eminent botanist John Lindley, who told him without the slightest hesitation that the flower was a previously unknown species of orchid. News that the first tropical orchid, named the *Cattleya*, had flowered in the most unlikely of circumstances created a sensation. Orchids had not, however, yielded all their secrets and propagation remained a complete mystery – their minute seeds (the smallest in the plant world) appeared to be sterile. Although an English grower, John Dominy, had managed through pure chance to germinate seeds obtained from the hybridization of two different species, it was not until 1909 that the Frenchman Noël Bernard discovered the secret of their germination. It emerged that microscopic fungi which live in symbiosis with the plants enabled the seeds to germinate. Orchids are now propagated in their millions, and thousands of *Cattleya* hybrids have been created.

Following pages : *Miltonia* 'Faribole la Tuilerie'. Family : Orchidaceae.

1 *Dendrobium* ×. Family : Orchidaceae. **2** *Dendrobium phalaenopsis* 'Pompadour'. Family : Orchidaceae. **3** *Vanda sanderiana* 'Terry'. Family : Orchidaceae. **4** *Odontocidium* 'Arthur Elle'. Family : Orchidaceae. **5** *Vanda rothschildiana*. Family : Orchidaceae. **6** *Phalaenopsis* ×. Family : Orchidaceae.

Opposite : *Phalaenopsis* 'Lady Amboin'. Family : Orchidaceae.

1 *Cymbidium* ×. Family : Orchidaceae. **2** *Vuylstekeara* 'Stamperland'. Family : Orchidaceae. **3** *Vuylstekeara* 'Cambria Plush'. Family : Orchidaceae. **4** *Paphiopedilum* ×. Family : Orchidaceae. **5** *Miltoniopsis lyceana*. Family : Orchidaceae. **6** *Odontioda* 'Menuet'. Family : Orchidaceae.

Opposite : *Paphiopedilum* × 'Allright Nadir'. Family : Orchidaceae.

1 *Dendrobium* × 'New Guinea'. Family : Orchidaceae. **2** *Ascocenda* 'Pralor'. Family : Orchidaceae. **3** *Dendrobium* ×. Family : Orchidaceae. **4** *Doritis* ×. Family : Orchidaceae. **5** *Odontocidium* ×. Family : Orchidaceae. **6** *Cattleyatonia* 'Jamaica Red'. Family : Orchidaceae.

Opposite : *Vandaenopsis* 'Désir Michel Viard'. Family : Orchidaceae.

Following pages : *Epiphyllum* ×. Family : Cactaceae.

1 Buddleia 'Lochinch' *Buddleia* ×. Family : Loganiaceae. 2 White Lilac *Syringa* ×. Family : Oleaceae. 3 Hebe *Hebe buxifolia* ×. Family : Scrophulariaceae. 4 Buddleia *Buddleia* ×. Family : Loganiaceae. Buddleia is native to Tibet, but when it was introduced to the rest of the world it was not long before it spread beyond the gardens where it was originally cultivated. In towns, as soon as space is cleared, buddleia moves in, growing on every building site and piece of waste ground. Botanists call these types of plant anthropophiles (meaning human-loving). In the countryside buddleia is a magnet for butterflies. In the midday heat it can be seen swarming with them as they come to extract the sweet nectar from the bottom of its corollas by means of their proboscis. 5 Hebe *Hebe* ×. Family : Scrophulariaceae. 6 Lilac *Syringa* ×. Family : Oleaceae.

Lilac is such a common garden plant that it is hard to believe its exotic origins. It was first identified in Turkey in the sixteenth century and subsequently introduced to Italy, France, Belgium and the rest of Europe, where it became naturalized. Until the nineteenth century, only two varieties were known, including the very rare white lilac. However, the discovery of a Chinese species, *Syringa oblata*, and a double-flowered variety led in 1876 to the creation of the first hybrid.

Opposite : Phlox *Phlox* ×. Family : Polemoniaceae.

1 Calceolaria *Calceolaria herbeo hybrida*. Family : Scrophulariaceae. Because of its unusual shape, this plant is also known as the "slipper flower". **2** Gloxinia *Gloxinia*. Family : Gesneriaceae **3** *Streptocarpus*×. Family : Gesneriaceae. **4** African Violet *Saintpaulia ionantha*. Family : Gesneriaceae. The African violet is easy to grow as a house plant and its small white, pink, blue or mauve flowers are produced all year round. **5** *Malope grandiflora*. Family : Malvaceae. **6** *Streptocarpus*×. Family : Gesneriaceae.

Opposite : African Marigold *Tagetes erecta*. Family : Compositae.

1 Pyrethrum *Pyrethrum* ×. Family : Compositae. Flowers of the *Pyrethrum* genus are used in the manufacture of natural insecticides, such as rotenone. **2** Cineraria *Cineraria cruenta*. Family : Compositae. **3** Hemerocallis or Day Lily *Hemerocallis* ×. Family : Liliaceae. **4** Cineraria *Cineraria cruenta*. Family : Compositae. **5** Helenium 'Beauty' *Helenium* ×. Family : Compositae. **6** Nicotiana *Nicotiana affinis*. Family : Solanaceae. The flowers of the nicotiana open in the evening, releasing a pleasant and long-lasting scent. The species from which tobacco is obtained has pink flowers and a much headier perfume.

Opposite : Californian Eschscholtzia *Eschscholtzia californica*. Family : Papaveraceae. A rather clumsy name for such graceful flowers, named after Dr Johann Friedrich Eschscholtz, who discovered them during a Russian expedition along the Californian coast in 1815.

1 Nasturtium *Tropaeolum majus* ×. Family : Tropaeolaceae. The nasturtium is an ideal flower for the weekend gardener. The less attention they receive, the more beautiful they are. For many years, nasturtium buds pickled in vinegar were used as a substitute for capers, sometimes without the consumer's knowledge. The flowers and leaves can be eaten raw. **2** Canna *Canna* ×. Family : Cannaceae. **3** Ixia *Ixia* ×. Family : Iridaceae. **4** Arum Lily *Zantedeschia* ×. Family : Araceae. **5** Amaryllis 'Stassen Glory' *Hippeastrum* ×. Family : Amaryllidaceae. **6** Abutilon *Abutilon* ×. Family : Malvaceae.

Opposite : *Kniphofia* ×. Family : Liliaceae.

1 Water Lily 'Arc-en-ciel' *Nymphaea* ×. Family : Nymphaeaceae. **2** Water Lily 'Greensmoke' *Nymphaea* ×. Family : Nymphaeaceae. **3** Water Lily 'Rembrandt' *Nymphaea* ×. Family : Nymphaeaceae. **4** Water Lily 'Albert Greenberg' *Nymphaea* ×. Family : Nymphaeaceae. **5** Water Lily 'Virginia' *Nymphaea* ×. Family : Nymphaeaceae. **6** Water Lily 'Texas Down' *Nymphaea* ×. Family : Nymphaeaceae.

Opposite : Water Lily 'Jack Wood' *Nymphaea* ×. Family : Nymphaeaceae.

In Antiquity, it was thought that the water lily destroyed the pleasures and narcotic effects of love. Along with lettuce, it is regarded as the ultimate anti-aphrodisiac and has long been used to dampen the flames of sexual desire. It was grown in monastery gardens to protect monks from the temptations of the flesh, and in rural areas was given to troubled children to cure them of their erotic dreams. In fact, recent research has revealed that the roots, which are very rich in starch, have rather more stimulating and tonic effects. The many species of water lily are of greater interest today for the magnificent, brightly coloured hybrids produced by cross-pollination.

INDEX OF SCIENTIFIC NAMES

INDEX OF COMMON NAMES

INDEX OF BOTANICAL FAMILIES

The author would like to thank all those who kindly assisted him
with the photographs :

Vincent Cerutti for the cacti
Jean-Claude Duformentelle for the orchids
Gérard Malinvaud for the aquatic plants
Roger Rousseau for the roses
**Jean-Claude and Louise-Marie Schryve for the bulbs
and other rare plants.**